Return to Essence

How to Be in the Flow and Fulfill Your Life's Purpose

Gina Lake

Endless Satsang Foundation

Endless Satsang Foundation

www.radicalhappiness.com
www.endless-satsang.com
ginalakenow@aol.com

Cover Photo: MichaelShake@dreamstime.com

Copyright © 2007 by Gina Lake

ISBN 978-0-6151-4119-0

CONTENTS

Who You Are—The Flow—The Ego and the *I*—The Life Plan—Discovering Essence

The Ego's Opposition to the Flow—Ego-Identification—Not Believing the Flow Exists—Turning Away from the Flow—Being Identified with Thoughts—Being Identified with Beliefs—Letting Fear Rule—Being Identified with Feelings

Discovering the Flow—Choosing to Be in the Flow—Meditation—Inquiry—Becoming Aware of Your Thoughts—Becoming Aware of Your Feelings—Identifying Your Stories

PREFACE

The understanding contained in this book was given to me by my inner teacher, who has guided, taught, and inspired me since 1990. I could not have written it alone because it describes the nature of life. Metaphysical truths require metaphysical teachers.

G. L.
February, 2007

INTRODUCTION

When you are in the flow, you know it. It does feel like a flow—like moving through water, going with the current. It's easy. You feel light. You're having fun. The flow feels magical because it is mystical. *The flow is the experience of who you really are as it moves through life.* It is the experience of essence—your true self. Once you experience this enough, you don't want to go back to not being in the flow. But how do you get there and how do you stay there? That is what this book is about.

To answer these questions, you first need to be clear about these two very different states—being in the flow and not being in the flow. The one you are probably most familiar with, not being in the flow, is dominated by the egoic mind (i.e., the ego-driven mind), which is the cause of suffering and difficulty. The other is the domain of essence, the divine within you. We will be exploring each of these in depth and how they interact.

You are meant to live in the flow, and when the time comes, you start experiencing it more and begin asking questions like, "What was that, and how do I experience that again?" The answers you get come from essence, and they come through your intuition, through others, and through books like this. When you are ready, as they say, the teacher appears. The Source has perfectly designed your existence to wake you up out of the egoic state of consciousness and return you to essence. That is what we are about here, so let's begin at the beginning...

CHAPTER 1
The Nature of Life

Who You Are

There is only One, and that One is you. You are a human manifestation of the Source. You are not apart from it but part of it. You are not just connected to it; you *are* it. You are not the whole of it, however, because there are many other manifestations. Everything you see and sense and so much more is a manifestation of the Source. Everything is it in disguise.

Why the Source does this is not so difficult to understand when you examine why you do things. Much of what you do, you do simply for the joy of doing or the joy of creating or the joy of experimenting. This is also why the Source does what it does—for the joy of doing, creating, and experimenting. There is immense pleasure in seeing what will happen when you do this or create this or try this. You feel this joy, which is the Source's joy in you.

For the Source to experience this joy, it had to create the possibility for experience, which it accomplished by creating manifestations of itself to interact with. For this to be as interesting as possible, it created great diversity and uniqueness, for what would be the point of duplication? Why duplicate an experience? If you look around, you see that the Source is infinitely capable of creating diversity. It delights in it. No creation is a disappointment or a mistake. Each and every one results in joy and also contributes to the Source's evolution.

The Source is constantly changing and evolving, just as you are. "As above, so below," the saying goes, and it is very true. You experience change, growth, and evolution, and so does the Creator. It created what it did to experience just that, so it should be no surprise that change, growth, and evolution are so much a part of life. Without these, what would life be? Very dry and uninteresting. And what would be the point of experience if it didn't provide these things?

The Flow

Many wonder what the point of existence, of experience, is. The point is the joy of experience itself—the joy of doing, creating, and experimenting and the wisdom and growth that come from that. You love to achieve new levels of understanding, expertise, beauty, creativity, and love. That is the Source's enjoyment as well and its motivation for doing, creating, and experimenting.

This joy can be experienced in any moment. It is an ever-present quality of the moment. The joy of the Source permeates life. It is tangible. It is real, and it propels life forward. *The moment—the now—is like a river, which carries you forward, ever-changing and ever moving. You either flow with this now or reject it and fight it, but that doesn't stop the flow; it only determines your experience of it.*

When you glide along with the flow, the experience is joyous, as you are able to experience the Source's joy in the moment it has created. When you fight the flow, you experience tension, anger, and dis-ease. You can't be happy when you are fighting the flow because you are too busy fighting it to experience the joy. You can only be happy when you are gliding along with the flow because happiness is synonymous with agreeing with the flow, with saying yes to it.

Just saying yes is not enough if this yes is a resignation—a reluctant giving yourself over to the flow. This is a step in the right direction, but too often this is a stopping point, one that leaves you joyless. To experience the joy and happiness available in any moment, agreement with the flow must include a real willingness to have the experience of the moment. You not only need to say yes to the flow, you need to embrace it. You must love it.

Loving the flow is the secret to happiness. The first step is saying yes to it, even if you don't feel that yes fully. Being willing to say yes to it can lead to a real feeling of yes. That is where your free will comes in—you can choose to say yes to the flow even when you don't like it.

Loving the flow is not dependent on liking it. It is much easier to love the flow when you realize that it is okay to prefer that something else be happening. *Loving the flow only requires that you jump into that moment—whatever is happening—and experience it fully, whether you like it or not.* The Source loves *experience*, and that is all you need to learn to love if you want to be happy.

The Ego and the *I*

Happiness comes from loving the flow, from giving yourself to it fully. This is easy to do when you like what you are experiencing but not so easy to do when you don't.

Who is this *you* that likes or dislikes an experience? The Source obviously doesn't have such preferences. It welcomes every experience, even unpleasant ones, or it wouldn't have created or allowed them. Unpleasant experiences are equally interesting and valuable to it and sometimes even more interesting and valuable because of the challenge they present to this *you* who is resistant to them.

This *you* that you think of yourself as coexists with essence—the divine in you—and usually overshadows it so that you come to think of yourself only as this *you*. However, the Source, as essence, is never apart from you. It breathes you and moves you, although its subtle presence is not very apparent. Its expression in your life often goes unnoticed.

The Source created this *you* to be a protagonist in the drama of life, for without conflict and opposition, how could it have a multitude of experiences? It needed to create a protagonist who is at odds with life and others in order to experience a variety of situations. When authors or screenwriters create characters, they create juicy ones, full of flaws and contradictions and with many different perspectives and talents. What will happen when they encounter others or face certain situations? The Source wants to know this, just as you do when you are taking in a good novel or movie. *What is it like to realize that your uniqueness and flaws are not a mistake but serve both the Source's and your personal evolution?*

The ego—that sense of your being a separate entity rather than at one with the Source—is not a mistake. The Source programmed everyone with a distinct personality, which is driven by an ego and supported by a unique mind and body. The ego is the sense of being *you*, of existing as an individual with distinct desires. Desires are central to the ego. It makes choices based on whatever desires are currently foremost.

These desires are always changing and nearly always contradictory, so this makes for the drama in life: In one moment, you choose one thing, and in another, you choose something else. Meanwhile, others are making their choices, which are often in conflict with their own and others', and their choices are constantly changing as well. Desires fuel most of the activity on earth and result in the evolution of consciousness, as you learn and grow from the consequences of your choices.

The ego—this sense of being *you*—is programmed to feel real. When you say "I," you really believe that you are speaking about someone. Very few stop to question the reality of this *I*, but what is it really?

Exercise: Finding the *I*

Stop a moment and try to find the *I*. Can you locate it anywhere? You may point to your body when you say *I*, but this *I* is not just the body is it? Does it reside in the body? If it resides in the body, then what is it that is aware of your body and your thoughts and even able to contemplate this question? Could that be who you really are? Is this awareness—this consciousness—limited to the body or the mind? *What if you were this awareness, and you were just pretending to be attached to a particular body/mind for the experience it provides consciousness?* Who would you be then?

These questions can wake you up out of the illusion that you are the *I*—an individual who has certain beliefs, thoughts, tendencies, desires, memories, and dreams. The *I* is deeply involved with and defined by the stories it spins about itself, but really, all the *I* is, is stories about itself, which are generated by the mind.

The real you is not your body, your mind, your personality, or any of the things you call yourself. What are these labels after all? They are just ideas. Are you an idea, or are you what is aware of the ideas, labels, thoughts, desires, and feelings of a particular body/mind?

The *I* is made up of ideas, and these are constantly changing, which makes for a very unstable self image. This *I*, which you call yourself, is imaginary and fluid. It is based on current stories about yourself and memories, which are also made into stories. These stories are just more ideas and have no intrinsic reality. They could just as well be replaced with other stories. They are the spin the ego gives to experience, and this spin is often very far from the truth because no story can contain the whole truth.

The truth is much simpler than any story you could tell. *The truth is that there is no true story you can tell about an experience.* Anything you say paints the experience in a certain light. Any story represents a perspective that emphasizes some aspects of the experience and de-emphasizes others to build a case. The question is: Build a case for whom? The ego, of course.

All stories serve the ego's purposes. They maintain, shore up, or protect the self image, which the ego sees as primary to its survival. All stories are designed to help the ego achieve its goals, particularly the goal of survival because, above all, the ego is a mechanism for survival.

To this end, the ego is programmed to seek pleasure and avoid pain; hence, its constant drive to make experience pleasurable and reject all experience that is not pleasurable, according to its definition. Essentially, the ego is in the business of rejecting life, except in those rare moments when it agrees with it; but even then, its next move is to try to improve on that. It is never satisfied with what is but always seeking a better moment or trying to avoid something in the present moment. This underlying discontent with life is caused by identification with the ego, which is ceaselessly dissatisfied.

The Life Plan

Most of the ideas and desires that come out of the mind are in service to the ego and its goals, and they drive life forward along a certain path, or destiny. Everyone has a destiny—a plan that is programmed into and carried out by the ego and its servant, the mind. This programming includes personality traits, desires, and drives that help determine and shape your choices, which lead to certain experiences and, hopefully, learning and growth.

This plan entails possibilities and potentials without predetermining the exact outcome. It makes certain choices and experiences more likely and others less likely, but it doesn't determine what specific choices will actually be made. That is determined by free will.

This life plan can be read in the astrology chart, which represents your personality, desires, drives, talents, and weaknesses. The Source is able to create a unique experience for itself by programming everyone uniquely and by providing other factors, such as environment, that will contribute to having an experience unlike it has ever had before. The ego is part of the programming and provides the sense that you really are this individual.

You also have a sense that you have free will, which is true from your perspective. You do make choices. However, these choices are often predictable because they are based on your programming, so free will is not as free as it may seem. Because of your programming, your choices are likely to fall within certain bounds. Astrologers have a saying: "Character is destiny," meaning that the personality traits and drives you are programmed with through astrology determine the types of choices you are likely to make, and those choices determine your destiny, or the life you create.

Although programming makes some choices more likely than others, no one is programmed to make bad or so-called evil choices. These come primarily from a lack of wisdom, and wisdom can only be gained through lifetimes of experience. Those who have had fewer lifetimes make more bad or evil choices than those who have lived more lifetimes because they haven't learned to make better choices yet. Wisdom is only gained through experience, and those who are not wise have not had as many experiences. This doesn't make them bad people, only inexperienced people who make bad choices.

Discovering Essence

There comes a point in your evolution when it is time to realize the truth about life and about who you really are. This point comes only after many, many lifetimes have been lived guided primarily by the ego, the mind, and the desires and conditioning programmed into the mind. This ego-driven mind will, from here on, be referred to as the *egoic mind*. After many lifetimes in the grips of the egoic mind, you begin to seek spiritual understanding and have more frequent experiences of *essence*, or the Source as it is expressed within you. There may be many more lifetimes at this stage in evolution, in which you continue to seek and begin to wake up to the truth about who you really are.

This waking up process is slow because your programming continues to have considerable influence until you have had many experiences of essence through meditation, other spiritual practices, or other means of expanding your consciousness. With increasing experiences of essence comes a loosening of the tendency to view yourself as the ego, the mind, the body, and the personality. Meditation and expanded states of consciousness give you an experience of essence—of the Oneness that you are—and you begin to identify with that instead of with the egoic mind and the personality. You begin to see your personality as a temporary costume you have donned to have this physical experience, while knowing that essentially you are a spiritual being.

This knowing eventually deepens into a shift of identity from the ego and personality to essence—to the Source within you. When this shift in identity happens, we say that you have *awakened*. This is a huge milestone in your evolution because now essence can more easily express itself through your body, mind, and personality and act more purely in the world, or less adulterated by the ego. Before this, it watched on and allowed choices to be made by the ego and expressed itself only intermittently and briefly through you.

After awakening, essence is more able to express itself through you without the interference of the egoic mind. It uses your personality to express itself because that is a necessary costume, or interface, with the world. Your personality doesn't disappear after awakening; it just becomes more fully a vehicle for essence.

As essence expresses itself through your personality, the personality becomes freer of its negative tendencies. The negative conditioning (programming) connected to the personality becomes less compelling. It becomes easier to see it for what it is and not become caught up in it. Detachment from the conditioning and the desires and demands of the ego develops, and these no longer run your life or determine your activities.

Essence is freer to make choices within your personality structure, and it uses this vehicle to fulfill its intentions in the world. Now you are living more in alignment with the intentions of essence than with your conditioning and ego-drives, and life goes much more smoothly. Your will (the ego's will) has become "Thy will."

Life is infinitely easier once you reach this stage of evolution. When you are aligned with essence, you feel the joy of the experience of the moment, and you naturally say yes to it. You know essence is infinitely trustworthy, so you just relax and enjoy the ride. When you know yourself as essence, you can just enjoy whatever happens.

You no longer demand that life be pleasurable or comfortable or fit any other idea. Unpleasurable and uncomfortable are equally wonderful experiences when you are in touch with the joy of essence. This lack of demand that life be a certain way is freedom. You are free to enjoy life as it is, whatever way it shows up. It was the ego that believed that life had to be a certain way for it to be happy and for you to be successful. It was wrong. Life can be however it is. Happiness is not dependent on circumstances but on saying yes to whatever is arising in the moment—pleasurable or unpleasurable.

Words such as pleasurable and unpleasurable, good and bad, comfortable and uncomfortable are evaluations of the mind, which create the very experience they define. They are stories told about an experience. If there is no such evaluation of experience, then experience is just what it is. That is what you eventually come to see as you awaken to the truth of who you are.

CHAPTER 2
Challenges to Being in the Flow

The Ego's Opposition to the Flow

Eventually you will live in the flow nearly constantly. Until then, you experience it to a greater or lesser degree, depending on a number of things. A big challenge to being in the flow is not recognizing that it exists because, without this awareness, you can't willingly choose to be in the flow over not being in the flow. You could say that the default position is to not be in the flow because that is the state of ego-identification, which is the usual human condition. Being identified with the ego ensures that you will not be in the flow or not be in it for long because the ego's reason for being is to keep you out of the flow.

The ego was created and programmed for that purpose. Being the protagonist of this drama called life, it is opposed to the natural flow of life, which takes you through both wonderful and not-so-wonderful experiences. The ego rejects most experiences and relates to the flow as if it were in combat with it. Its basic stance is to reject whatever is happening and attempt to change it—to either improve on what it likes or get rid of what it doesn't like.

The Source intends to have a variety of experiences through everyone, and it has also programmed everyone with an ego that automatically opposes whatever is being experienced. This creates the suffering in life. So you could say that you are programmed to suffer, that is, until you awaken. You are not doomed to suffering. In fact, this very suffering is what eventually wakes you up.

Suffering could be defined as the ego's opposition to whatever is. This opposition creates an underlying discontent with life, which makes it difficult to experience the joy and happiness that are available in every moment. How can you experience this joy when the ego keeps you so busy evaluating life and devising plans to change or improve it? These activities keep the mind busy nearly constantly, and when you are identified with the mind in this way, you are divorced from the actual experience of the moment.

This detachment from experience and involvement with mental constructs puts you in a made-up reality created by the mind. This reality is full of reasons why things are not right and how they could be better (evaluations and judgments), dreams and imaginations of how things might be, comparisons between the present and the past, beliefs about how things should be, desires for things to be different, rehashing of past events, and mental rehearsals for some future moment in time. Feelings generated by all this mental activity are part of this made-up reality; and they, in turn, generate more thoughts and more feelings.

This mental world is the world most people live in most of the time, and it is not real. It doesn't have the solidity and juiciness of real life, of living in close contact with the aliveness and joy of the moment. This can only come from saying yes to life instead of no.

Saying yes allows you to be present to whatever is happening in the moment. Saying anything but yes instantly puts you into identification with the egoic mind, which immediately spins a story and sets up a plan of action to either improve on or do away with something about the current reality. This can keep you very busy and tends to structure most people's lives.

Think about it. What do you spend your time doing? How do you decide what to do with your time? Isn't this usually determined by an idea about how something could be better? This is not to say that this should not be happening, because you are here to have experiences, and the Source allows you to make the choices you do because it enjoys having whatever experience you choose. However, some choices lead to more happiness, freedom, and fulfillment than others. The choices that are driven by the ego do not lead to these things.

There is another possibility, and that is to allow essence to spontaneously choose what you will do moment to moment. This spontaneous choosing comes out of the moment, though, so you won't find these choices in the mental world of the ego. They come out of the flow; and for you to choose them, you must be in the flow and not in the ego's made-up mental world.

Ego-Identification

People want to be happy, and they generally believe they will be if they do what the egoic mind suggests. That is the trap and the great misunderstanding because that is a prescription for unhappiness, not happiness. *You are programmed to think that happiness lies in a direction other than it does.*

Searching for happiness in all the wrong places (e.g., success, money, fame, relationships, beauty, eating, sex, and pleasure) creates challenging and interesting situations, growth, and considerable pain. The Source intends these experiences and this growth. It also intends that you discover the true source of happiness eventually. It intends that you discover who you really are, but until you choose to do that, there is great richness in the human drama and even in the suffering.

Learning, growing, discovering, creating, gaining wisdom, and developing talents and positive qualities are intrinsically rewarding, even if suffering is required to accomplish them. These are the rewards of being fully involved in the drama of life and ego-identification. The Source is not a sadist who enjoys the experience of suffering. What the Source loves and celebrates are the many priceless gifts that come from suffering: wisdom, compassion, kindness, understanding, patience, love of peace, love of freedom, appreciation for life, inner strength, generosity, and faith, to name a few. These gifts often can't be obtained except through suffering, not on this physical plane anyway. They give richness and meaning to life. So, even lives that are lived in full ego-identification have their rewards and their purpose.

True happiness is too simple and ordinary for the ego. The ego would rather feel the high of an addiction than the contentment of the moment. It seeks thrills and extreme sensations and feelings. The happiness and joy of the moment is too subtle to be appreciated by the ego. It finds contentment and joy boring and uninteresting, and uses that as an excuse to turn to other things—to the world of thought.

More than anything, the ego wants to feel special, and what comes out of the moment is more like Oneness than specialness. The happiness and joy that come from being in the moment are the result of recognizing essence and your Oneness with all that is. It is quite the opposite of the happiness the ego feels when it achieves what it wants, which usually is something that makes it feel special or superior to others. The ego's worst nightmare is to not exist as a separate entity, which is the main reason it turns away from the moment and from essence.

The experience of essence is very frightening to the ego and of no value to it. Therefore, it is invested in rejecting the moment. It discounts and overlooks the joy of the moment and the subtle experience of essence, which can only be felt when the mind is quiet. The ego is extinct when the mind is quiet, so it wants to avoid that. Thoughts draw attention away from essence and bring you into the realm of ideas, beliefs, judgments, dreams, memories, desires, and feelings, which is the world the ego survives and thrives in. It can't exist outside of this mental world, so it seeks to draw you into its world.

Angels and devils is a good metaphor for this duality between essence and the ego. This duality feels like you have an angel on one shoulder and a devil on the other, each whispering in your ear. Of course, the ego is not a devil, and it is not even separate from the Source, which created it to do just what it does; but this duality serves to create the human drama and ultimately to awaken you to your true nature.

The suffering created by being separate from essence and aligned with something opposed to it (the ego) eventually results in a longing to return Home—to return to a condition of love, peace, joy, and contentment. Brief experiences of these pure states fuel this drive to return to essence. As you evolve, you have more experiences of these qualities of your essential nature, and entrancement with the egoic mind is loosened. Then you begin to question more the nature of life, why you suffer, and who you really are.

You begin to realize that two possible conditions exist: the state of ego-identification and the experience of essence. This is a very important and necessary recognition. Without this, ego-identification will continue to be the state that life will be lived from most of the time because that is the state you are programmed to reside in until you awaken.

Not Believing the Flow Exists

If the ego is not who you are and it doesn't have the answers to how to live, then what does? Is there something else? Some get stuck here and decide there isn't anything else. When they go looking for something else that guides their lives, they find nothing and give up. However, no-thing is exactly what is guiding life. This nothing that is found is actually something; it's just not a thing.

When you ask Who am I? you find nothing but space, but this spacious nothingness is actually who you are: You are not a thing. What you are and what is capable of guiding your life is not something you can sense in the way you sense objects. It belongs to another dimension and requires other-dimensional sensitivity.

Since you are a multidimensional being, you are capable of sensing essence, but it doesn't feel like the physical self that you usually identify with. Essence is experienced when you are in the flow, which happens when you are very present to the moment, and it has the qualities of the flow: love, peace, acceptance, compassion, contentment, happiness, clarity, wisdom, and joy. When you are experiencing these qualities, you are experiencing essence.

To be in the flow and stay there requires acknowledging that such a thing exists. For many, this requires a leap of faith. They are afraid they will lose their way if they acknowledge something they can't understand or prove. They often need encouragement from those who have already leaped. The Source has helpers in the form of those who have gone before, who help those who are not quite as far along. Some stages in evolution can only be bridged by others showing the way. The Source has ways of introducing its helpers to those who are ready to take this leap of faith.

Turning Away from the Flow

To be happy, it is not enough to acknowledge that the flow exists. To live in the flow, you need to *commit* to living in it. This is a big step—from acknowledging the flow to committing yourself to it. It's not so easy to stay in the flow once you get there because the programming to turn away from it is very strong. To counter this programming, you need to engage your will.

Up to this point in evolution, your free will has not functioned that freely. Your choices have been shaped primarily by conditioning—by the particular programming you received. For the most part, your will has been synonymous with the will of the ego. Once you begin to wake up out of the illusion spun by the egoic mind and its programming, another kind of will comes more fully into play—the will, or intentions, of essence.

Although essence has always been involved in shaping your life, it becomes more predominant and actively involved once you become more aware of it. You begin to coordinate your personal will with essence's intentions, and your choices more often reflect essence. The dance between essence and the ego is led now more by essence than by the ego. Ultimately it will become a dance between the awakened individual and essence.

Essence's intentions are different from desires. While desire has a specific goal, intention has a broader target. Essence has general intentions rather than specific desires. It intends growth, it intends learning, it intends manifesting certain qualities (e.g., love, peace, kindness, and generosity); and it allows you to choose specifically how these intentions will be brought about.

You have always had the choice of following essence's intentions or the ego's will; however, your programming causes you to follow the ego's will without questioning its value or validity. You don't ask: Is what I'm driven to do in this moment true? Is it in the highest good of everyone concerned? What is it serving? You just do it and meet with the consequences. Fortunately, these consequences eventually cause you to evaluate your choices and ask these questions.

Asking these questions can wake you up from ego-identification and bring you into the flow. Commitment to being in the flow is crucial because without this, you will probably act without questioning the ego's motives, which are primarily self-serving. This self-serving activity is very unfulfilling and causes a lot of pain for everyone. Yes, it creates the drama of life, but the purpose of the drama is to evolve you, wake you up, and bring you back to essence. The pain of the drama eventually brings you to the flow because peace and happiness exist there and nowhere else, and that is what you really want, not what the ego offers as prizes.

What is it that questions the ego's drives and choices if not the ego? These questions don't come from the ego because it is not in its interests to undermine its own strategies and goals. What else is there?

Even when you are deeply enmeshed in the egoic state of consciousness, essence is active in your life, and it asks these questions. It draws you to itself by asking these questions. It coaxes you but allows you to continue to be led by the ego if you choose. *The waking up process is a slow one because you always have the choice to go back to ego-identification. In every moment, there is a choice to be made: Do I agree with the egoic mind and follow the ego's drives and desires, or do I follow something else?* This is where commitment comes in.

Being Identified with Thoughts

The biggest challenge to being in the flow is being identified with thought. Thinking is not actually the problem but rather your relationship to it—whether you are identified with it (i.e., believe it) or not. Thoughts will always arise in the mind, and not all thoughts are a problem. Some are inspired by essence. However, most thoughts represent the programming you were given, which maintains the sense of *I* and the egoic state of consciousness. Most thoughts are superfluous to living and only interfere with happiness.

The ego is nothing if it isn't the mind. The ego is created and sustained by thought. *When thinking stops or is simply ignored, identification shifts from the ego to essence.* This is why meditation is important for those seeking freedom from ego-identification. Meditation and other techniques that quiet the mind or cultivate detachment from it can help you be in the flow and stay there.

Being aware of your thoughts is the antidote to identifying with them. You don't have to stop thinking or do away with your negative thoughts to be happy and aligned with essence; you only have to stop responding to your thoughts. This aware detachment allows you to see what is true about your thoughts. What you discover is that there is very little true about them.

Until you interrupt identification with your thoughts by distancing yourself from them, you will find them interesting and compelling, and you will assume they are true and useful guides for your behavior. You are programmed to believe this about your thoughts. Without this, it would be impossible for the Source to play out the roles it is playing. However, there comes a time for these roles to be taken over by essence and for essence to move this character (you) as it chooses, not as the ego chooses.

When this time approaches, you find yourself questioning your thoughts more: Where do they come from? Is that true? Why am I thinking this? You become weary of having the same thoughts come up repeatedly. You learn about psychology and the unconscious, and you encounter spiritual perspectives that cause you to question your long-cherished beliefs and attitudes. You begin to get free of some of your conditioning, perhaps through therapy or meditation, and this freedom is exhilarating.

Once you have a taste of freedom and of the peace of essence, you don't want to go back to ego-identification. Being identified with the ego is painful, and you have discovered that the ego's solutions to this pain are short-lived and unsatisfying. You want more. You long to discover the secret of life—the secret to being happy. So, the search for the Truth begins.

Being Identified with Beliefs

Beliefs are deeply held patterns of thought that structure experience. You believe something, so you behave accordingly. Most activities you choose to engage in are based on your beliefs. For example, if you believe that education is necessary to compete in the world, you go to school and study hard. If you believe that having a family will give meaning to your life, you have children. You *do* things that are in alignment with your beliefs. Those who have different beliefs and values spend their time doing different things. These differences make the world go around. Everyone is programmed with different beliefs.

These beliefs and values are rarely questioned, and when they are, it creates an identity crisis. Beliefs are very tied to identity—to the sense of who you are: I am someone who believes in Christianity. I am someone who believes in eating right. I am someone who believes in having fun. Beliefs form the basis of identity. Without these, who are you? How would you describe yourself? Even your roles reflect your beliefs: If you are a mother, you believe in motherhood. If you are a teacher, you believe in education. Roles reflect your beliefs and the identity you have formed around them.

Beliefs keep identity intact. When beliefs change or are questioned, identity changes or comes into question. That is why challenging someone's beliefs can feel so threatening. The ego is defined by such identities and roles, and without these, it is nothing. Beliefs create and maintain the ego.

As with thinking, beliefs themselves are not the problem but rather your relationship to them. Identifying with your beliefs causes identification with the ego. Another possibility exists, and that is to have beliefs but not be attached to them. *It is possible to notice the beliefs and opinions that arise in your mind without taking them personally—without thinking of them as yours. You see that they belong to your body/mind and are part of the drama your body/mind is living out but that they are not who you are or necessarily a useful way to structure your life.*

Each belief you hold needs to be examined for its validity and usefulness. Many will be seen as false and having never been useful, some will be seen as having been useful but not useful now, and others will be seen as useful now, at least for the time being.

Most beliefs set you apart from others, and that is the state of ego-identification. When you are identified with a belief, a judgment, or any other thought, you have created a *you* who believes such and such, who is at odds with everyone else who doesn't believe such and such. However, if you see that a belief is just another thought and you hold it lightly, it doesn't have to interfere with enjoying others, their differences, and their beliefs.

Separation from others and from life is the primary experience of the ego, while Oneness is the primary experience of essence. *Since no belief can contain the whole truth, no belief is the ultimate truth. Beliefs are just not worth fighting about. They aren't worth the separation from others and from essence that they cause.*

The more lightly you hold your beliefs, the easier it is to not feel separate from others. Those who hold their beliefs strongly can then seem endearing to you, as you understand that they are embroiled temporarily in identification. You feel compassion for the pain they create for themselves by doing this.

In recognizing that beliefs, opinions, and judgments are a primary source of separation from essence and the way the ego is created and maintained, you are free from them. You can still choose to follow those that create more love, peace, joy, and happiness for you and others, but you are free from the pain of separation that most beliefs create.

Letting Fear Rule

Fear is the mechanism used by the ego to keep you tied to your thoughts and beliefs and consequently to the egoic state of consciousness. It is the weapon the ego uses to bind you to itself, and it is what needs to be overcome to be free of ego-identification. Fortunately, this is not as difficult as it sounds. After all, fear is just another idea, and like all ideas, it has no reality. How difficult is it to overcome something that has no reality? Overcoming fear is only difficult if you give fear reality by believing in it.

Fear is a creation of the ego. If you examine any one of your fears, you will see that it is referring to a future possibility, not a current reality. Fear is almost always tied to a negative idea about something in the future that hasn't happened and probably won't happen. It is the emotion that is generated by thinking about some dreaded possibility in the future. This emotion becomes fuel for activity designed to vanquish what is feared. Many of your activities are responses to fears. These fearful thoughts are particularly difficult to ignore or detach yourself from because you feel your survival might be at stake if you don't take them seriously.

Some warnings are worth heeding, of course, but much of the fear that drives human behavior is based on a false idea. For example, you are afraid you won't be loved if you don't look a certain way, so you go to great lengths to have a certain appearance. This fear drives you to do a lot of things that are essentially unnecessary. Being loved is not dependent on how you look.

Many false beliefs exist that are fueled by fear (e.g., If you don't kill terrorists, they will kill you). They are responsible for a great deal of the suffering on earth. They cause suffering not only because being in a state of fear is painful but because this state of fear and the activities that come from it keep you from being in the flow and experiencing the joy that is available right now, in this moment. You also might miss out on doing more fulfilling things that would be in the flow because you are too busy with fear-based ones.

You think the ego plays a useful role in keeping you safe, but it doesn't. *The flow can be trusted to keep you safe because out of it comes true wisdom and insight about the present moment.* It guides you to act appropriately in this moment, and those actions will be ones that support your survival and safety (assuming that is essence's intention). The flow is eminently trustworthy and has everything you need to be happy—and safe.

The ego wants you to believe otherwise because that gives it an opportunity to be the one that structures your life. This gives some reality to its unreal existence. If you didn't pay attention to the ideas it spews and act on them, it wouldn't have a sense of existing. The ego does have something to be afraid of because if you see the truth—that it doesn't exist—it loses its reality.

Being Identified with Feelings

Another challenge to being in the flow and staying there is feelings. They, like ideas and beliefs, are generated by the egoic mind and can't exist or be sustained without thought. Ideas and beliefs—including unconscious ones—fuel feelings, and feelings fuel actions. Feelings can be very compelling. Often more ideas and feelings arise to fuel the initial ones, and before long, an idea has solidified into a *story,* which is a point of view that leaves out many aspects of the situation. When this point of view bumps up against another, more feelings are generated, and so it goes. If this process weren't behind most thoughts, relationships would be much simpler.

The mind creates stories around ideas that you are identified with, and these stories precipitate feelings and then actions. Thus, you can become very busy as a result of your thoughts. This process perpetuates the egoic state of consciousness. The story is always in service to the ego in some way. It upholds the self image, a belief, a way of life, or something else you are identified with. The story maintains the idea of an *I* in the midst of plenty of proof to the contrary.

Without the story, there would be no *I.* The stories you tell about yourself are made-up. They could be anything, but your story goes a certain way because you are programmed to see yourself in a particular way. Your self image, which is just an idea, is part of your programming, and your stories are designed to explain this image to others and to yourself. You feel some comfort in being able to describe yourself in a certain way, even if it is not a very happy story. At least it is a story. At least you exist. The ego is afraid of the nothingness that is your true nature. When that is experienced, it runs back to its thoughts and stories. No matter how terrible they may be, they seem better than nothing.

When you are experiencing a feeling, such as anger, sadness, depression, hatred, jealousy, or shame, it is a sign that you have bought into an idea. You have become identified with a particular way of looking at something—with a story. This story is what causes your pain, not anything in your experience. The story creates painful emotions, and then you move farther away from experiencing the whole truth of the experience by trying to justify these emotions and the actions that follow from them with more stories. Around and around you go, stuck in your particular perception of experience.

Being in the flow is much simpler. *When you are in the flow, you experience whatever you are experiencing without telling a story about it. Thoughts may arise, but you recognize them as thoughts, as an attempt on the part of the ego to define the moment because that is what it tries to do. Meanwhile, you just stay in the experience of the moment, which is forever morphing into something else. When you are in the flow, you know yourself as that which is aware of the thoughts, not someone who is thinking them.*

Watch the mind as it tries, in every moment, to co-opt experience by translating it into a story. It tries to draw you away from experience into a mental world that simulates experience. It tries to draw you into an imagined story about the experience. If it succeeds, that story becomes your experience. If you agree to go to this mental world, feelings will also arise and add reality to this world, but it is still a mental world. Once you act on these thoughts and feelings, you create new experiences.

In this way, the ego does manage to shape your life, and this will go on as long as you allow it. Most people's lives are shaped nearly entirely by the ego. Essence allows this because it enjoys the growth that results, but this way of living is full of suffering. Essence offers other possibilities for your life, which you may miss if you are not in the flow.

CHAPTER 3
Overcoming the Challenges to Being in the Flow

Discovering the Flow

Being in the flow is your natural state. What could be more natural than experiencing your true nature—essence. When the mind is quiet for a moment or stopped by something of beauty, for instance, you find yourself automatically in the flow, where you find peace, happiness, contentment, and joy.

The flow is not just a pleasant place to be, however, where nothing happens; it is infinitely intelligent and alive. Motivation, action, communication, creativity, insight, inspiration, vision, ideas, and wisdom all arise from it. Life happens, and it happens the way it happens. All of life comes out of the flow, and it does so easily and spontaneously.

It is possible for your life to be lived from this place rather than from the mind, and it is a very different experience. So let's look at what you can do to live more in the flow.

You are already familiar with the flow and probably experience it many times a day, at least briefly. It is easy to recognize: It feels good! Anyone who performs at his or her peak is familiar with what it feels like to be in the flow: Athletes know it, artists and musicians know it, writers and speakers know it, performers know it. However, you don't have to be at the top of your field to experience the flow. You can experience it right now.

Exercise: Finding the Flow

Just stop and give your attention to what is going on right now, without evaluating it or commenting on it. Just *be,* without thinking. If a thought or desire arises, just notice that and come back to just being. What do you notice? This moment is packed with experience. Input is coming in through your physical senses and through more subtle ones. What are you experiencing in your body? What are you seeing? What are you hearing? What are you smelling or tasting? Notice all of these things without reacting to them, evaluating them, or telling a story about them. If feelings arise, just notice them as well. If you don't become engaged with them, they will simply disappear into the same emptiness that gave birth to them.

What else is there besides sensations, thoughts, desires, or feelings? What else do you sense with your more subtle senses? The peace, joy, and contentment of this moment are sensed with more subtle senses than you are used to using. The more you use them, the more they develop and the more real the subtle world becomes. When you are fully sensing the moment this way instead of being in your thoughts about it, you are in the flow.

Notice how this moment—this flow—is always changing into something else. What is arising now in this new moment? Urges for action also arise and things happen, so in the next moment you may find yourself doing something rather than just being. Doing arises from the moment without thinking. This is an amazing experience when you first become aware of it.

Choosing to Be in the Flow

The flow is simple and ordinary. Because of that, it is overlooked and underrated by the mind, which will try to convince you that there is nothing in the moment worth paying attention to. It entices you to pay attention to it with thoughts about the present, past, and future. You must choose.

Exercise: Choosing the Flow

Notice how uninterested the mind is in the present. It is fascinated with the past and the future, and it likes to evaluate the present, but it finds nothing of interest in the actual *experience* of the moment. Notice this. Notice how persistently it makes suggestions for thinking about something or doing something other than just being in the moment and expressing what is coming out of that. It has a job to do, and that job is to keep you out of the moment. Notice how clever it is at doing this. Notice all of its tactics. How does it attempt to do this? It is programmed to do this, and it does a very good job.

Now that you have seen this, you can be free of its manipulations. You are free to choose: You can give your attention to the moment and see what it has to offer, or you can follow your thoughts to where they take you. At some point, you become tired of doing the latter and ready to find out what else is possible. What would your life be like if you didn't follow your thoughts? What would you do? What would you choose? What would you say? When you are in the flow, doing, choosing, and speaking still happen, but they come out of essence rather than the ego.

This choice must be made moment to moment. You can't just make this choice once and be done with it. *You must make this choice to give your attention to the moment again and again until being present in the moment becomes automatic and your natural way of being.* Making this choice takes an ongoing commitment to waking up and allowing essence to live through you.

To make this commitment, you have to want this. You have to want to be done with the ego-based existence more than you want to be a someone with a story. Suffering is a strong motivator. However, those who make this commitment usually do so because they also have had enough tastes of essence to know what it is like to live in the flow. It's just too painful to go back to ego-identification after experiencing that.

Meditation

Meditation is the way many have come to know essence. Others have come to know it through art, music, sports, or other activities that are totally absorbing. Whenever the mind is occupied through focused attention, essence can be experienced. Activities that require one-pointed focus provide a doorway to essence. The more experiences you have of essence, the easier it is to experience it and the more motivated you are to make it your constant experience.

Initially in any meditation practice, there is resistance on the part of the ego to sitting quietly. This is the last thing it wants to do. It is helpful to just notice the egoic mind's resistance and accept it. Of course it feels this way, but this doesn't have to interfere with taking time to do this. Commitment to being in the flow may require commitment, first, to a practice of meditation. This will help build a bridge to essence that will make it easier for you experience it more and for longer periods of time. In meditation, you are training the mind to take a backseat to essence, and like any type of training, this takes time, effort, and repetition.

Exercise: A Simple Meditation

Wherever you are, just listen. Notice the sounds around you without reacting to them, evaluating them, or thinking about them. If judgments or thoughts arise, just notice those. If feelings arise, just notice those. If the urge to get up and do something else arises, just notice that for the time being. Now, just listen, as if that is your sole task in life. Give your attention fully to the sounds around you.

Even after just a few minutes of this, you will feel more present, peaceful, and alive. This aliveness is who you are. This is essence. When you feel this aliveness, you know you are aligned with essence. Do this whenever your mind feels busy, confused, or overwhelming.

Inquiry

Inquiry is another technique to help you experience and align with essence. If you have never experienced essence for more than a flash, inquiry can bring about a very profound experience. It uses the mind to stop the mind, to bring it to a place where it can't go. The mind is not capable of grasping essence, which is not a thing. That is one reason it is not interested in it. The mind not only has difficulty perceiving essence, it doesn't understand it when it does encounter it. Essence is too unknowable for the mind. No words can describe it, so when the mind encounters it, it stops briefly. Then it tries to get you to go back to the world of things, for which it was designed.

Because inquiry is so simple, it is easy to overlook its power to return you to essence. It seems too simple to bother with, but that simplicity is its strength. Because it is so simple, you can apply it in any moment, and it takes only a moment. The reward is that it interrupts the egoic state of consciousness and makes room for the possibility of being in the flow.

Exercise: Inquiry into Your True Nature

Begin by asking the question Who am I? What answers arise in response to this? Examine each to see if they are true. Are you your body? Are you your history? Are you your personality? Are you your social roles? Are you your goals? Are you your talents? Are you your mind? What are you? Who is this *I* that you call yourself? What do you find when you look for it?

You probably couldn't find an adequate answer to the question Who am I? and you couldn't find any *thing* that is you when you looked for it. This is the correct result. There is no answer and there is no *you.* You, as you *think* of yourself, does not exist. What does exist then? What remains?

This consciousness, this awareness, this no-thingness, this spaciousness, this emptiness that you find is who you really are. You are this Nameless One. The essence of all of life is right here, and it is aware of and unfolding your life right now in this moment. Nothing else has ever really been living your life but this. There has only been an appearance of a separate someone who is living this life and experiencing this moment. In reality, there is only *experience,* and you are that!

Becoming Aware of Your Thoughts

Most people don't question their thoughts, and many are not even aware of them. Their relationship to them is: "This is what I think." They express these thoughts and act on them, and this becomes their life and who they are. The opinions, beliefs, ideas, perspectives, memories, dreams, and desires (which are also thoughts) of the *I* is who they seem to be—not only to themselves but to others, who are equally involved in their *I.*

This is not really a problem if you don't take these thoughts so seriously, as if they are the right ones. They are just thoughts—the thoughts of your particular body/mind. They reflect your particular programming. They help make you the unique person that you are, and this uniqueness makes life interesting.

This programming is not a mistake. It provides experiences that lead to growth. Nevertheless, it is possible to have more pleasant and fulfilling experiences through your particular body/mind by being less identified with its programming and more identified with essence. Dis-identification with your programming can only come about, however, if you are first aware of it.

Exercise: Cultivating Awareness

Who you are is Awareness. Awareness is another word for essence because awareness is a quality of essence. You are that which is aware of whatever you are aware of. You are aware of reading these words right now. How do you experience this Awareness? Does it have an energetic feel to it? Some call this Awareness "Aliveness" or "Awakeness" because it feels alive and awake. Some call it "Consciousness." This Awareness is always present: You are never not aware. Even when you are asleep, when you wake up, you are aware that you slept.

You can learn to live in identification with this Awareness rather than in identification with thoughts, which is the state of ego-identification. All it takes is becoming aware of that which is aware of a thought or a feeling or a desire, or that which is aware of thinking, feeling, or desiring.

You can choose to become aware of a thought at anytime. *Waking up from the trance of ego-identification is a matter of choice. You choose to notice the Awareness, the Awakeness, the Aliveness that you are. Thoughts still arise and pass. You may even get involved in thinking, but you don't have to lose awareness of yourself as awareness of all that is happening, including thinking.*

One of the qualities of this Awareness is curiosity. When you are aligned with essence, it is an experience of loving, nonjudgmental curiosity. When you feel this detached but loving curiosity, it is a sign that you are no longer in ego-identification. On the other hand, judgment (which is a thought) is a sign that you are in ego-identification.

Becoming Aware of Your Feelings

Becoming aware of your feelings is easier than becoming aware of your thoughts because feelings are less subtle and often difficult to ignore. You can't choose to not have a feeling once you have one. However, you can choose to be aware of a feeling you are having and experience it rather than ignore or deny it; and you can choose what you will do as a result of that feeling. Usually feelings drive behavior: You feel something and respond automatically, either internally with thoughts and more feelings, or externally with actions.

There is another possibility, and that is to simply experience the feeling and allow it to be there. If you give it your curiosity and attention without doing anything else, you will find out something valuable about it. Behind every feeling is a mistaken thought or belief, or possibly an entire story, which is responsible for triggering the feeling. Feelings are real sensations in the body, but unreal thoughts cause them. You can learn to trace a feeling back to the thought or story behind it. This can free you from the feeling and eliminate any need to act on it. Once you see the mistaken idea behind a feeling, the feeling loses its power to drive your behavior. *Most behavior that is motivated by feelings is at the very least unproductive, and much of it is damaging.*

For example, you may think you need to tell people when you are angry with them. Many are taught to deal with feelings this way. However, a better way of dealing with anger, or any other emotion, is to take responsibility for creating it and look for the mistaken belief underlying it. You are responsible for your feelings; other people or circumstances are not. *Your feelings are caused by what you say to yourself about a situation.* Nothing else. The proof is that not everyone has the same reaction to a situation. A situation that may make you angry may not make someone else angry. There must be something else going on, and that something else is your belief system—your conditioning.

You can learn a great deal about your conditioning this way. Moreover, you can free yourself from it because when conditioning is seen repeatedly, it eventually stops showing up.

Exercise: Uncovering the Conditioning Behind a Feeling

Every feeling has something to teach you about your conditioning. The next time you experience an uncomfortable feeling, such as anger, sadness, depression, hatred, jealousy, or shame, instead of brushing the feeling aside, feeling bad about it, expressing it, or acting it out, try doing the following:

Be very present to the feeling, as if it were a child having this feeling who you wish to understand and support. Become very curious about the feeling: Why is it there? What idea (either conscious or unconscious) might be responsible for it? Once you discover what is behind it, ask: Is that true? You will find that the answer is nearly always "no."

Being present to feelings and uncovering the misunderstandings or false beliefs behind them will allow you to be more present to the situation that triggered them. From this place of presence, appropriate action or non-action will arise out of the flow.

One of the most common misunderstandings that fuels anger is the belief that things or people *should* be a particular way. This is always untrue because things can't be different than they are right now. "Shoulds" are ideas—opinions—imposed on reality. They give anger impetus and make it feel justified. If things *should* be different, you feel justified in fighting them, trying to change them, complaining about them, even harming someone over them.

Acting out your anger won't improve any situation. If there are any steps to be taken to improve the situation, these steps will be much easier to see and more productive if they are not colored by your anger. When you drop into the moment by being very present to a feeling and the belief behind it, clarity is possible, and from this clarity, positive action may arise.

Identifying Your Stories

People don't just have ideas and self images; they have stories. These stories come up repeatedly in internal self-talk or conversation with others. They are easy to identify: Like any story, they have a beginning, a middle, and an end, and usually something tragic about them. Most have a "poor-me" or "isn't it awful" quality about them, but others serve to glorify the self. Some change or disappear over time, while others endure for a lifetime.

The stories you are most identified with have strong feelings attached to them. They have an emotional charge that you and others feel when you tell them, and they tend to trigger emotionally charged stories in others. This often becomes the basis for relating to others, the means of sharing.

Sharing this way is often thought of as intimacy, but this is a false intimacy because it is a sharing of the false self—the ego. True intimacy is a sharing of yourself from the level of essence. This is a totally satisfying experience, accompanied by love, joy, acceptance, and peace. When you are in essence, it feels like all is right with the world and with others. The feeling is the opposite when you share yourself from the egoic level through a story. It is one of contraction and tension, and negative feelings and fear are usually stirred up within yourself and others.

It is important to identify the stories you tell about yourself because they keep the ego alive. They keep you identified with the *you* that you are pretending to be rather than with essence. In getting over your stories, the hurdle is not in identifying them, because that is easy to do, but in breaking your attachment to them. People *love* their stories. They love them because they give the ego a sense of reality and, particularly, a sense of being special. Both tragic and heroic stories serve this purpose. They give you a sense of being a unique person—and you are. There is nothing wrong with being unique, but you are not special in this uniqueness, at least no more than anyone else.

Exercise: Getting Free of Your Stories

Notice the energy around *I* when you are talking with someone. When you say *I*, it is usually charged with emotional excitement. The *I* loves to talk about itself. It can hardly wait until the other person is done before it explains how it is for itself. When you feel this energy around *I*, you can be sure that it is a story. You can use these cues to become free of your story. Notice what makes up the story because that will tell you about your conditioning, and also notice the energy behind it. What is that? What is behind that energy, that drive, to speak about yourself? That is the ego.

Once you see the story for what it is—the ego's attempt to be special—it becomes easier to let it go. However, you have to see this and be willing to let it go. You have to be willing to forgo the payoff of being special. What do you get in exchange? You get your real self. You return to essence. Once you experience this enough times, it is not so difficult to let go of the story. Resting in essence is much more pleasant than ego-identification. Being identified with the ego and its stories doesn't feel good. You love your stories *and* they make you suffer. When you are done with your stories, the reward is the peace and love you were seeking all along.

CHAPTER 4
Getting into the Flow

Recognizing the Flow

The flow has the qualities of essence because the flow refers to the flow of essence, which is not static. Who you are— essence—is not a thing but an ever-changing and ever-evolving *experiencing*. When you look for who you are, you will never find someone or something who is having an experience; you will only find experience, awareness, consciousness. You are awareness of experiencing, but you will never find someone or something that is aware. Consciousness is another word that points to who you are, but you won't find someone or something that is conscious.

This experiencing or awareness or consciousness is easily taken for granted because it is like the air you breathe: It is so ever-present and subtle, and you are so immersed in it that you don't notice it. It seems like the *I* is experiencing, aware, conscious, but this is a false conclusion. *You are programmed to feel that there is an experiencer that you call I. However, when you look, you see that the I only exists as an idea. It is not experiencing, aware, or conscious.*

The flow is recognized by its qualities, which are qualities of essence. When you are in the flow, or aligned with essence, you feel one or more of the qualities of essence. The most commonly present qualities are love, peace, happiness, joy, and acceptance. In some moments, other qualities of essence stand out, such as wisdom, clarity, compassion, and strength. These other qualities are still always present, but they are often less prominent.

From moment to moment, the qualities of essence that are predominant change, depending on what the moment calls for. If it calls for clarity, that arises. If it calls for compassion, that arises. If it calls for strength, that arises. Essence provides whatever is required in any moment. These qualities often go unnoticed because when you are identified with the ego, your attention is on the mental world and not on what is flowing out of essence. In addition, these qualities are subtle and energetic and not experienced by the five senses.

These qualities can be experienced on the egoic level as well; but when they are, they are diluted and distorted by the ego and are mere reflections of the qualities of essence. Their pure form is only experienced when you are in contact with essence. When you are identified with the ego, you get tastes of happiness, joy, peace, and love, but these are tainted by self-interest or won at someone else's expense. When you are identified with the ego, what makes you happy, joyful, peaceful, accepting, and loving is getting your way or achieving some goal of the ego. However, because the ego pursues things that can never result in true happiness, real happiness will never be experienced in the egoic state of consciousness.

Occasionally, the ego's goals do coincide with essence's, but more commonly they are at odds with the nature of essence. The ego wants to feel superior, and it wants what it wants at all costs. This is the opposite of what makes for true happiness, so the ego is unable to achieve happiness except briefly. As soon as it does, it begins devising a new goal, and it will not be happy until it achieves that. Then if it succeeds, it will be happy briefly, but soon it will become dissatisfied with that, and the cycle continues. The egoic state of consciousness is a state of dissatisfaction, with only brief glimpses of satisfaction and happiness.

The ego is programmed to seek happiness in ways that can never produce it. Instead, its agenda leads to unhappiness and constant restlessness and dissatisfaction with life. Fortunately, essence has a way of penetrating the egoic state. Everyone has at least brief moments of true happiness, love, peace, joy, and acceptance. This is what makes it possible for you to wake up out of the egoic state. You eventually discover ways to elicit the experience of essence, without perhaps even realizing what you are experiencing.

Experiencing the Flow in Extraordinary Moments

Certain activities evoke essence, even when you are deeply identified with the ego. Generally, these are moments of being fully absorbed in something. This absorption can take place while doing very simple, mundane activities or by participating in exhilarating, life-threatening ones. Any moment has the potential for this level of absorption, but certain circumstances make it more likely.

When your life is threatened or you need all of your resources to perform a task—when you are stretched to your limits—this absorption is natural, and essence presents itself, often taking over the activity you are engaged in. When essence expresses itself through you this way, it is very fulfilling, and you experience the qualities of essence, especially those that are needed at the time.

These moments have been termed *peak experiences*. They stand out in memory because of their degree of presence and aliveness, which are qualities of essence. This aliveness is not like any other egoic experience. It has a depth and richness that is inherently fulfilling, and that fulfillment evokes joy.

The Source rejoices when you return to essence, and this joy can be felt. This joy is not the usual joy, and yet it is simple, plain, and ordinary—free of the grandiosity and self-focus of the ego. The ego's joy is giddy and infused with a sense of all-powerfulness and pride. The joy of essence, on the other hand, is experienced as Oneness and connection with something greater than the personal self. Selflessness, not self-centeredness, is the experience along with a feeling of not being able to take credit for any good you have done.

Those who are considered heroes nearly always describe the heroic act as something they just did without thinking. They often recount that they feel like *they* didn't do it and therefore can't take credit for it. This is similar to what you often hear from artists, musicians, writers, athletes, or others at the top of their field when they are asked how they are able to do what they do. Many of them feel that something else takes over and is to be credited for their accomplishments.

This something else is essence. When this happens, it is called "being in the flow." It seems miraculous and extraordinary when it happens, but it is actually possible to be in the flow nearly constantly. Many do live in the flow much of the time, and some are not even aware of it. Those who are very high functioning in positive ways are likely to be examples of this. Being in the flow is such a natural state that it seems ordinary when you are in it most of the time.

Dropping into the Flow in Ordinary Moments

You don't have to be functioning at the top of your field or testing your limits to experience the flow. You can experience it in very simple, ordinary moments. *Whenever you are in touch with a quality of essence, even if it is just a sliver or reflection of the pure quality, that can be used as a doorway into the flow.* Sometimes just hearing someone say "love" or "peace" drops you into the flow because of associations with the love and peace of essence. This can also happen by being around those who are expressing a quality of essence. Essence can be contagious. Even movies and books that express qualities of essence can drop you into essence and the flow.

Love is the most obvious example of this: When someone or something evokes love in you, it is an opportunity to ride that love into the flow. This is one reason relationships are so valued: They offer an opportunity to love and to experience essence. Relationships also evoke lots of other things— judgments, fantasies, desires, stories, and other conditioning— which can take you out of the flow.

Being accepting, like being loving, is another simple thing you can do in an ordinary moment to evoke essence and bring yourself into the flow. Acceptance is a quality of essence, and when your attitude or behavior reflects that, you drop into essence and the flow. To stay there, you will have to continue to be accepting, but you can learn to make acceptance your natural response to life. The more you practice acceptance, the easier it becomes, although effort is needed at first to overcome the ego's automatic resistance to life and to whatever is happening.

Just resting and being quiet and still is another simple thing that can drop you into essence and the flow. Being still helps quiet the mind and relax the body, which brings you into peace, another quality of essence. By behaving peacefully, you evoke peace and essence.

This is true of any quality of essence: Simulating it or attempting to reproduce it as best you can, can result in a true experience of it. Any attempt to embody or express a quality of essence affirms your desire to be in the flow. Using your will in this way is like a prayer—a call to essence—and when you are sincere and allow room for essence to appear, it will. *So, if you want to experience love, peace, or acceptance, act loving or peaceful or accepting, and essence will follow.* The motive needs to be pure, of course. You act in these ways because you want to be aligned with these qualities, not for selfish reasons.

Beauty is another thing available in simple moments that can bring you into essence because it naturally evokes love. Beauty has a way of opening the Heart and causing you to say yes to the moment. This yes brings you into essence and the flow for as long as you allow yourself to experience the beauty and the moment instead of listening to anything the mind has to say about it.

Being absorbed in a sensory experience is another easy way to drop into essence and the flow. The senses are doorways into essence because when you are fully involved in seeing, listening, tasting, or feeling sensations, without thinking about the experience or telling a story about it, you will find yourself in essence. This is why sex has often been described as "the little death." Full involvement with this sensual experience can evoke a sense of Oneness, which is a quality of essence.

Anything you become fully absorbed in can bring you into essence and the flow. What absorbs you, if not things you love? When you love an activity, you are likely to experience the flow for as long as you are engaged in it. This is why many enjoy hobbies, games, music, dancing, art, and sports so much. When you are absorbed in something you love, you experience pleasure and a certain ease in doing it, even if it is challenging. This pleasure and ease are hallmarks of essence.

When you are in the flow, life feels good and easy. You are not struggling against the moment, just flowing with it, without questioning it or evaluating it. The mind interrupts experience with thoughts *about* experience. It brings you into its world, which is a world of doubt, worry, fear, separation, judgment, and confusion. When you are experiencing these, you are identified with the ego, not essence.

Fear, judgment, negativity, and confusion are signs that you are not in the flow. They point to the need to make another choice. *Once you know about the flow and how the mind keeps you from it, it is up to you to choose to be in the flow. No one else can do that for you. Essence will wait until you decide to choose it over the ego, the flow over fear.*

Being Present to the Moment

Every moment presents an opportunity to be in the flow if you pay attention to it. Attention is the key to being in the flow.

Whatever you give your attention to, is what you identify with. If you give your attention to the products of the egoic mind—thoughts, feelings, or desires—you will become identified with the egoic mind. If you give your attention to the *experience* of the moment—to everything that is arising in the moment from the position of Awareness—you will be identified with essence.

The reason this is not as easy as it sounds is that you are programmed to give your attention to the products of the egoic mind. You were programmed this way because this is how the illusion of being a separate entity is maintained. The Source created this illusion so that it could have the experience it is having through you, but it also intends for you to wake up from it eventually.

When you stop giving your attention to your thoughts and other products of the egoic mind, the *I* dissolves because it is seen for what it is: ideas about *I*. The *I* can't be sustained when you are actually present to what is going on in the moment because the *I* is only a thought. If you are present to the moment, you are not thinking (but rather being present to any thoughts), and there is no *I*. See for yourself. As soon as you start thinking, the *I* is in nearly every thought: I want, I like, I am, I feel, I think.

Exercise: Just Being

When you are just being, who are you? Who you are feels more like consciousness or awareness or being than *someone*. There is a sense of relief in just being without being someone. This sense of relief is a sign that you are in essence. You relax from all your striving to be someone, particularly a better someone. When you are fully present to the moment, you discover a world where there is delight in just being. Isn't that what you have been wanting all along? How funny to find it right here in this simple, uncomplicated moment.

Being present to the moment is actually very pleasurable. It is much more pleasurable than ego-identification, but you won't convince the ego of that. Because the *I* can't be sustained in the present moment, the ego wants nothing to do with being in the moment. It wants you to return to its fabricated mental world, where it is king. If you listen to it, you will leave the experience of the moment because the egoic mind is compelling. It was designed to be compelling.

When you realize the egoic mind's game, you are at a choice point. Where do you put your attention? *If you want to wake up out of the illusion and the suffering created by the egoic mind, you have to choose to not go where it wants you to go. You must choose this again and again, in every moment, until it becomes a choiceless choice, one that is automatically made out of love for essence. With repeated experiences of essence, it becomes increasingly easy to choose essence.* Even so, there will be times when your conditioning will be too compelling to ignore, and you will find yourself back in the mind and ego-identification.

Being present in the moment is a matter of noticing what is going on. It is an attitude of receptivity to what is. This receptivity is not passivity or a cold objectivity but more of a loving curiosity: Let's see what is happening now. Curiosity is a quality of essence, and being curious—even faking it at first—will drop you into the flow.

This curiosity is free of judgment and evaluation because those belong to the egoic mind, not essence. This curiosity accepts whatever belongs to the moment, including the ego not liking something about the moment. This curiosity is interested in whatever is just because it is. That's all. It accepts it without conditions or demands that it be any other way and without opinions about it. Thus, a preference for things to be different would be one more thing that essence would accept about the moment.

There is room in this acceptance for everything—even non-acceptance. When you are in the flow, the foreground is acceptance, and the background may be non-acceptance. When you are identified with the egoic mind, the opposite is true: You are paying more attention to the non-acceptance of the ego than the ongoing, natural acceptance of essence.

Acceptance is a natural outcome of being in the moment, and you can cultivate it by saying yes to whatever is arising. This can become a spiritual practice, which will make acceptance more automatic.

Exercise: Saying Yes to the Moment

What is arising now in this moment? Try saying yes to that. Notice what else is arising, and try saying yes to that too. Is there anything about this moment that you could not say yes to? Even if you don't like something about it, could you just let it be here? Saying yes to something is just letting it be here. *You don't have to like it. You just have to allow it to be here— for now.*

Saying yes to something is not going to make it stay or make it go. It has no effect on whether something stays or goes. What it affects is your *experience* of the moment. *Saying yes to whatever belongs to this moment helps you stay in the moment and appreciate it. This moment will never be duplicated—it will never come again. For that reason, it deserves your allowing and honoring. Allowing is the natural state of essence. When you allow, you return to essence or remain there.*

Allowing is a place of humility, of not presuming something is good or bad or that you know how this moment should be. Notice how sure the ego is about its opinions about what is happening. Is it usually right?

Being Present to Whatever You Are Doing

Sometimes what is coming out of the moment is activity: You are doing something. These moments are likely to be more common than moments of non-activity. Like every other moment, moments of activity are opportunities to be present and in the flow.

In the egoic state of consciousness, activities are chosen based on the ego's values, goals, and drives. Many activities are based on conditioning—things you think you should do. Some of these are very necessary and worthwhile, but many are a waste of time and energy. People spend enormous amounts of time and energy doing things that don't give them true happiness or improve the quality of their lives or the lives of others but only serve the ego. For example, accumulating unnecessary things and taking care of them consumes a huge amount of people's time in this society. The egoic mind leads people down paths that are ultimately unfulfilling, but that is part of what you are here to learn.

When you are engaged in an activity in the egoic state of consciousness, you are usually thinking about something else. If this were not the case, you would drop into the flow, and you might not even decide to do that activity. If you really allowed yourself to experience the activity you were engaged in, you would either find yourself enjoying it or, from the place of essence, you would choose differently. Either is a much better outcome than not being present to what you are doing and not enjoying it.

It is possible to enjoy any activity, even things you prefer not to have to do, if you are fully present to it. Whenever you are doing something, much more than just that activity is coming out of the moment, and that can be a source of joy at any time. For example, if you are washing the dishes and you are very present to doing that, you will notice many other things than your supposed dislike for this activity: the warmth of the water, the sparkles of the soap bubbles, the depth of the night sky through the window, the shadows made by the folds of the dishtowel, the sloshing sound made by the water, the sweet tiredness of your body, the satisfaction of getting a necessary job done, and appreciation for the simplicity of the moment.

When you are present to what you are doing, you are rewarded by a quiet mind, or at least a mind that remains in the background. This is a great relief. You don't have to listen to the negativity, complaints, arguments, confusion, fear, worries, and old worn-out stories of the egoic mind. If they *are* there, they seem more like a bad radio station in the background rather than about you. They don't seem personal. Being present to what you are doing quiets the mind, and that is its own reward. Relief from the egoic mind and immersion in essence can turn an activity that *you think* is unpleasant into a very pleasant one.

When you have experienced essence in these ways often enough, it becomes apparent that *how you think about and define your experience determines your experience.* Since most thinking is negative and resistant to what is, not thinking is a definite improvement. Not defining an experience or telling a story about it (e.g., "I hate washing dishes") frees you to actually experience it, and any experience that is free of commentary from the mind is pure joy.

The Power of Meditation

Meditation is powerful for two reasons: It gives you the experience of essence and it trains you to drop into essence. Everyone has brief experiences of essence through the ordinary and extraordinary ways just mentioned, but they often remain brief because programming makes it challenging to remain in essence for long. Meditation counteracts this programming and creates new pathways in the brain that allow you to stay in essence for longer periods of time.

Meditation brings the mind under the control of something other than the ego. It allows you to take back the mind from the ego. The mind can be and eventually does become the servant of essence. Once this occurs, the mind is used when it is needed and quiet when it is not needed. Moreover, it no longer pretends to be who you are. Although it can take quite a while to attain this level of detachment from the mind, many have achieved it and were able to do this through meditation.

Meditation brings about a new relationship to the mind, one that is free of egoic interference. The mind functions perfectly well in this new relationship. You are able to function much better without all the trouble, conflict, and confusion the ego creates. The ego makes life much more difficult than necessary, while pretending to be of help. It creates problems and then ineptly tries to solve them. Something else is much more capable of living your life, and it has been responsible for much of what has happened, despite the ego's attempts to shape life. That something is essence.

Summary: Things that Bring You into the Flow

- Activities that stretch your limits
- Contact, even superficial, with any of the qualities of essence
- Simulating a quality of essence
- Affirming your desire to experience essence
- Love
- Acceptance
- Rest and relaxation
- Beauty
- Activities you love: music, art, dance, hobbies, games, sports
- Giving your full attention to seeing, hearing, sensing, tasting
- Any activity that fully absorbs you
- Allowing whatever is happening to be happening
- Being present to whatever you are doing
- Meditation

CHAPTER 5
What Makes the Flow Go

The Ego's Relationship to the Flow

The flow is always changing into something else. The moment never repeats itself or stays the same for long. This is a fact of life, which the egoic mind doesn't grasp, or doesn't want to. It is sure that whatever it doesn't like about the moment is not only a problem now but potentially forever. In those rare instances when the egoic mind likes what is happening, it assumes it should be able to make it last. However, your mind has never been able to affect the moment, only your experience of it. If you agree with your mind's story about the moment, your experience of it will coincide with that.

The truth is that anything you say about a moment leaves out more than it includes. It is therefore a partial truth (i.e., a lie), and a biased one at that. The egoic mind puts its own spin on the moment, defining it according to its conditioning, perceptions, and needs. Furthermore, this spin is usually a negative one, oriented toward what the moment lacks, not what it actually offers.

Moments are full of all kinds of things—colors, sounds, sensations, movement, activity, people smiling, people frowning, mail arriving, phones ringing, dogs barking, needs arising, thoughts, desires, feelings, intuitions, inspiration, drives, resistance, and qualities of essence. The egoic mind singles out one or two of these and spins a story.

For example, in the previous dishwashing example, the egoic mind might focus on the tiredness of the body and assert that there is something wrong or unpleasant about that, which needs to be fixed—and dishwashing is not helping! Or it may point out that the dishtowel on the counter should have been hung up ("Why don't the children ever do that!") or it is too wet or too dirty or the wrong color or too old. Rather than just noticing what is and loving it, which is the experience when you are in essence, the egoic mind complains and finds fault with whatever is. The dishwashing moment is what it is, but there are many possible experiences of it depending on what you decide to think about it.

Every moment has this same potential for being either okay as it is or not okay, depending on whether you are identified with essence or with the ego. Undoubtedly, you would prefer to be okay with every moment, but the ego convinces you that this is not okay either. It tells you that if you accept things the way they are, you won't be safe, you won't get anything done, you won't be successful, you won't be loved, you are lazy, you are stupid, and on and on. It will tell you whatever is most likely to take you out of the flow. That is its role. It is the adversary of the flow.

Exercise: Noticing the Ego's Tactics

Becoming aware of the egoic mind's tactics is an important step in learning to be in the moment and in the flow. Which tactics are the most successful at getting you to turn away from the moment? a memory? a fantasy? a desire? a fear? a should? a judgment? a thought about food, sex, time, imperfection, cleanliness, being successful, or how you look? Does it repeat this particular tactic or thought or try others? What does it do when you don't listen to it? How long do you actually stay in the flow before you go unconscious and rejoin the egoic mind? Does a particular tactic or thought cause this or do you just become worn down by a barrage of thoughts?

Get really curious about the egoic mind. It is fascinating to watch it as it attempts to manipulate you. Careful observation of it will help you become free of its domination and stay in the flow longer.

The Flow Has a Direction

The ego would oppose the flow whether the flow had a direction or not because the ego can't exist in the flow. It doesn't value the flow or see meaning in it. When you are identified with the ego, this becomes your point of view as well. You, too, find the moment to be pleasant or unpleasant, a problem or not a problem, but not necessarily meaningful or having anything of value for you. It seems dull, ordinary, pointless, directionless. As a result, it makes sense to try to make it more interesting and rewarding to you (the ego).

The egoic mind tries to move the moment in the direction it wants. However, it can never succeed because it has no power to affect the moment except symbolically—through thought and imagination. It imagines what it wants to be happening, but that doesn't make it happen, does it? Only in the imagination. The egoic mind can have what it wants through thought and only through thought.

You enjoy your fantasies, but in the end, they don't change what is happening now. Furthermore, when you are involved with them, you are not enjoying what is real. You might not care, though, because you may not know how to enjoy the moment because you haven't spent enough time in it to find out. So, people live in and, to some extent, enjoy their mental worlds. Fortunately, reality is always waiting for them when they return. Those who don't attend to the moment may return to a reality that is not so pleasant because reality does require attention.

Although the egoic mind doesn't notice or comprehend it, the flow does have a direction. There is method to its madness. The flow is going, and it is going somewhere. Where it is going is inspired by essence. The ego is allowed to co-create through free will, but the flow essentially belongs to essence and is directed by its intentions.

If it were not for points of consciousness like you, the Source would not have a way of experiencing the flow. *You are both a creation of the Source with its own individual destiny and a means the Source has devised to experience everything it has created. It not only designed you to experience the flow but to interact with the flow and co-create with itself.* What a plan, and what a blessed gift it is to be alive and have this opportunity!

The Source has overall intentions for creation as well as specific ones that support its overall intentions. Some of these are very general. For instance, the Source intends both physical evolution and evolution of consciousness, not only for humans but for all life forms. What is all this evolution moving toward? In a word—love.

On a human level, "love" includes what you think of as love, but it also refers to being aligned with essence and to fulfilling your potentials and chosen destiny. It refers to your gradual return to essence, which occurs as a result of waking up out of the egoic state of consciousness.

Waking Up from the Egoic State of Consciousness

This waking up process is a gradual one, which culminates in a shift in identity from ego to essence. This shift is often referred to as *awakening,* but waking up is likely to have begun long before this shift in identity, even lifetimes before. Some wake up more quickly, while others are more sluggish about it.

How quickly you wake up depends mostly on how you use your free will. You must choose essence over ego again and again before this shift in identity is possible. It makes no difference to essence how long this takes. Essence calls you toward itself, and everyone eventually answers this call.

The point of waking up is not to end your suffering, although that is the result, but to help end other people's suffering. The Source created you to evolve and then to be its hands, legs, eyes, ears, and mouths in the world. It created you to help others wake up. What some might need to get to this point is basic education. Others might need food. Others might need the kind of spiritual understanding that is offered here. The point is that assistance in many forms is needed to help those along who are suffering, and ultimately you were created for that.

You are most capable of offering the kind of help someone needs when you are aligned with essence because essence knows what is needed. Only then can you be a real servant of essence. Otherwise, you are a servant to your ideas about what someone needs, which may not be what is needed. Most likely these ideas are the ego's, which when it is educated, has lots of beliefs about how to help people, not all of which are true. Discovering how to serve well is part of your evolution. You come to realize that the best service comes from discerning what is needed in the moment and providing that. You can only discover this if you are in the flow and present to the moment rather than to your ideas about how to help.

The Life Purpose

Waking up is not always necessary to fulfilling your potential or life purpose. Many have a life purpose that does not involve waking up in this lifetime. There is a time for everything, and waking up comes in its own time. Nevertheless, everyone does have a life purpose—something the Source intends to accomplish through your particular body/mind and personality.

The Source intends for you to have certain experiences and to learn and accomplish certain things. As best it can, it programmed you to have the experiences, challenges, and resources you need to learn and grow and to accomplish what it intends. However, the Source's intentions are only a plan, not an edict. What happens in life is not predetermined, only preplanned, and you know how plans go! In this world, with free will and so many unpredictable variables, the outcome of each life is not known. It is not known how each plan will unfold specifically and whether the Source's intentions will be fulfilled. Perhaps something completely unexpected will be accomplished or learned. Perhaps nothing will. The Source doesn't know how each plan will work out. That makes life interesting for everyone.

Fulfillment in life comes from fulfilling your plan, regardless of what that plan is. People are fulfilled by different things, sometimes very simple things. Some destinies are very simple: learning a skill, learning to reason, learning to care for the body, learning to assert yourself. In your later lifetimes, you are destined for more complex accomplishments, but not in the earlier ones, when simple things must be learned and only simple things are likely to be achieved. From the Source's perspective, these lifetimes have just as much value as the later ones.

Your plan is encoded in your genes and through other means, including astrology. There is no better way to learn about your life plan than by getting to know your astrology chart. It is a powerful resource for understanding your personality, lessons, talents, strengths, weaknesses, psychological and past life issues, karma, and life purpose. The chart not only describes the programming and plan you were given, but how it is being brought about through your experiences. If you want to know more about these things, get your chart done by a good astrologer, one with both a psychological and spiritual perspective.

Fortunately, you don't have to know anything about astrology to fulfill your plan. You are being driven to fulfill it by the Source's intention. You can feel its intention when you pay attention to the moment. You won't find the answers in your mind for how to be fulfilled and happy. For this, the mind is more likely to confuse than elucidate (although it is useful for balancing a checkbook and following a recipe). *Your plan can be known by paying attention to the impulses, drives, and spontaneous actions and ideas that come out of the moment.*

Ideas that come out of the moment have a different quality than those that come from the egoic mind. They arise spontaneously and are not thought about, just acted on. They feel more like an inspiration to act than an idea. They are uncomplicated by the confusion and negativity of the egoic mind. Instead, they have a rightness and clarity about them, which makes them easy to act on.

At the same time, your mind has been programmed with your particular conditioning. The thoughts that come up in your mind are designed to be there. They are the grist for your mill. Your conditioning is what causes you to suffer, grow, seek understanding, and evolve. You have been given this conditioning to learn from it and overcome it. It brings you situations and difficulties that have the potential for teaching you so much, although what you learn or whether you learn from them at all is up to you.

Without your conditioning and the programming of the egoic mind, you would be in the flow all the time, and that is not actually what the Source intended. It intended that you not be in the flow until you learn to be in the flow. In a sense, you have to earn being in the flow by overcoming the obstacle to that—the egoic mind. Rather than being a mistake, the egoic mind is a tool for evolution.

What Moves the Flow

The flow is essence unfolding in the moment. The flow contains whatever is present in the moment, and what it contains is always changing. It moves toward some things and away from others. It includes some things and excludes others. It is always changing, but it changes for a reason. The flow has directionality. It moves in a certain direction because it is directed to either by essence or by free will. How it changes is not solely up to essence but also up to free will, which in most cases equals the ego's will.

Thus, the ego's will is part of the flow's direction, and for many, it is the main determinant of the flow's direction because essence allows the ego's will to shape the flow within certain bounds. Essence is interested in seeing what will be created, and it values the lessons that result from the ego's choices. Nevertheless, the flow's direction is ultimately under the control of essence, although it doesn't always choose to exercise that control. It often allows you to create whatever you choose, while continuing to try to influence you in ways it deems necessary. Usually, what happens in any one moment is a co-creation between your ego and other egos and essence.

Other egos are an important factor in the flow's direction. The direction of the flow is not only determined by your ego and by essence but by other egos as well. Some moments are an expression of a multitude of egos with many different desires. When that is the case, the direction might follow what the majority wills, or essence may move the flow in an entirely different direction. The more egos there are involved, the more volatile and unpredictable the flow's direction.

As a result, predicting anything but the very immediate future is difficult not only for people but for the nonphysical forces guiding them. Even the very immediate future can be difficult to predict. Free will is a real force in creation. It is responsible for much of what is created because that is how humanity is learning, and learning is the Source's intention.

Sometimes essence has specific intentions that require certain circumstances. When that is the case, essence will do what it can, usually through others, to create those circumstances. Essence can't manipulate things in the physical world except through people, so it requires cooperation from people to accomplish its goals.

Fortunately, getting this cooperation is not as difficult as you might think. Because most respond automatically to their thoughts, essence sometimes uses thought to serve its goals. People are easily influenced by suggestions planted in the mind, and many also respond to intuition. As a result, anyone might serve the intentions of essence without even knowing it.

Thoughts that come from essence have a different quality than most conditioned thoughts. They generally lack a feeling of personal investment and self-interest. They feel more like commands or urges to do something, and they are usually acted on spontaneously. When you help essence in this way, you feel good about having carried out the suggestion, although you may not understand why you feel good. That good feeling is your reward.

You don't always respond to these suggestions because you are free not to. Some suggestions are dismissed or just overlooked. When that happens, essence will try to find someone else to carry out its intentions.

Facilitators of the Flow

The Source has not only human helpers but nonphysical ones, who help shape human activities. Most often, nonphysical helpers do this by motivating you through your intuition or by planting desires, drives, or thoughts in your mind that will inspire particular actions. Not all your thoughts, desires, and drives come from the ego. Essence also uses the mind and desires to carry out its intentions, but more often than not, your thoughts and desires belong to the ego and are part of your conditioning.

These nonphysical helpers mediate between the Source and human beings via essence. They understand human beings and their propensities because most have been alive in a physical body. They evolved beyond the need for the physical experience and are now busy guiding human beings. They are learning too, and life is messy and unpredictable, so their guidance is not always effective, but they do their best to make the flow go in the direction that essence intends.

These nonphysical helpers are a manifestation of the Source (like you) and are evolving by performing their tasks and by being involved in lessons appropriate to their level of reality. There are helpers at every level of reality who are assigned to helping those who haven't reached that level yet. This is how the Source manages creation: Those who are more evolved help those who are less evolved, and everyone evolves as a result. This is also an efficient way for the Source to stay in touch with all that it has created. This hierarchy, if you will, also serves as a communication network: What is occurring on one level of creation is communicated to the other levels.

Those who are guiding your level have graduated from it. They awakened from the egoic trance and learned to live in alignment with essence. The qualities of essence are what they strive to continue to express in their work with you. Those qualities are love, wisdom, acceptance, tolerance, patience, kindness, compassion, peace, and sensitivity, to name a few. Beings who don't express these qualities in relating to you are not qualified to guide you. Such imposters do exist. They are primarily those who have died but not graduated, who take on a role of guide prematurely, usually for selfish reasons.

The Impact of Desire on the Flow's Direction

Desire has a big impact on the flow's direction. It is what lies behind and fuels the will. The Source allows desire to impact the flow's direction because desire is its tool for evolution. Desire brings the lessons about. In the egoic state of consciousness, a thought appears, a desire is generated, a story is told about what getting that desire will mean, that generates feelings, and those feelings keep the desire alive and fuel actions, which bring about consequences and ultimately learning. You learn to be creators by following a thought to its manifestation in the physical world. Many things can interfere with manifesting a desire, and that becomes part of the learning as well. Nevertheless, the process of desiring and then using the will to try to bring that about makes the world go around. It creates experience.

Since it is the Source's intention to have experiences through you, all of this activity is just fine with it. It allows you to create what you will; however, its approach is not hands-off. Through essence, it is intimately involved in what you are creating and using what you create to orchestrate situations that will develop certain talents and qualities (e.g., love and wisdom) and bring about certain lessons. Its intention is that you develop certain talents and qualities, accomplish certain tasks, and learn certain things, according to its plan for you within the experiences you are freely choosing. *Your free will creates the context within which the elements of the Source's plan are brought about.*

The Source holds all the cards, however, because you are programmed to develop certain talents, you are given conditioning that creates challenges that stimulate the growth and learning intended by the Source, and you are given drives that cause you to be attracted to certain activities more than others. So, although you have free will, the drives, desires, and talents that make you unique and motivate many of your choices are programmed by the Source.

So, if you are programmed to fulfill the Source's intentions, what interferes with this plan?

Blockages to the Life Plan

A number of things can interfere with this plan or cause it to go off course or even fail. Although not the biggest interference, free will is the most obvious one because you *are* free to go against your imprinting, you *are* free to not stay in the moment, you *are* free to follow your thoughts, you *are* free to not listen to your intuition or other impulses that are coming out of the flow. However, the egoic mind poses the biggest problem because it keeps you out of the flow and therefore out of touch with the plan for the most part, although there are still ways you can be reached.

When you are in the flow, the plan can be unfolded gracefully and happily because you are aware of what the flow is asking of you and where it is going. You are not trying to go against it, which is painful. When you are in the flow, you learn what you need to learn and grow in ways you need to grow and willingly contribute to life in the ways you were meant to. When you are in the flow, you are not resisting the plan, so it can unfold as easily as possible. Even if being in the flow entails some challenge or adversity, which it does at times, when you are in the flow, you have access to the inner strength and resources you need to successfully deal with that.

Challenges, and even adversity, are blessings in disguise because they develop your greatest gifts: inner strength, fortitude, courage, faith, compassion, patience, tolerance, love, acceptance, appreciation for life, to name a few. These are the gifts you get to leave this life with. You are here to develop these qualities, and often they are developed through adversity. You don't have to suffer during this adversity, however. Because of these gifts, even adversity can feel fulfilling when you are in the flow.

The ego keeps you out of the flow and identified with it rather than with essence by keeping you involved in its mental world, where life is not actually happening. The ego is trying to make life happen its way by holding ideas about life. It declares: "It should be this way, it could be this way, it will be this way, it has to be this way!" Sometimes it pleads: "I want it to be this way. Please make it be this way." It assumes (or hopes) these declarations and pleas have the power to make it so. It assumes that by managing life or finding just the right formula, it can make life be the way it wants it to be.

It takes a lot to convince the ego differently. The ego is never really convinced. Only by dropping into essence is it possible to see the truth about life and the falseness of the ego's world. Many lifetimes are lived caught up in trying to make life turn out according to your ideas, without seeing that this is not possible nor does it bring fulfillment or happiness. Eventually, essence bleeds through, and you get a taste of real fulfillment and happiness and a taste of freedom from the suffering caused by following false ideas.

By following the ego's ideas about how to live life, you can still learn a lot, so there is no harm done, and essence allows this. Sometimes the plan is modified if entrenchment in the ego is so great that the intended plan can't be fulfilled. In later lifetimes this occurs less frequently, however, as essence is more able to guide you through your intuition and your thoughts.

Because essence can penetrate the mental world of the ego with thought, it is able to reach into the egoic state of consciousness and influence your choices and begin to awaken you from this state. As you evolve, the intuition is also used by essence increasingly because it is more developed and more likely to be listened to than in earlier lifetimes.

Two real adversaries of being in the flow are conditioning and fear, which are part of the egoic mind. Either of these can be a reason for turning away from an intuition or a thought that would bring you into the flow. Many receive thoughts and intuitions that, if followed, could bring them great fulfillment and happiness, but they don't follow them out of fear or a belief (conditioning) that they shouldn't or can't follow them. Your conditioning causes you to have a certain self image, which is limiting. These limitations can be difficult to overcome without considerable encouragement from others because going against conditioning causes a lot of fear. You feel you might not survive—and your self image might not!

This is where helpers come in, in the form of others who offer encouragement to see yourself differently and to follow your intuition or do what feels right. When essence isn't able to reach you through your intuition or thoughts, then it will try to reach you through others who act as mouthpieces for it. This actually is a very common experience.

When this happens, there is a rightness about it, relaxation, relief, a big yes! When you hear the truth, you know it. *Being in the flow is actually the path of least resistance, but it doesn't seem that way when resisting life is what feels most natural. It can be scary to let go into the flow, to let life take you where it wants to take you, without questioning it, fighting it, worrying about it—but trusting it. That is a new relationship to life, and new ways of being are uncomfortable at first.*

The ego's need to control is a lack of trust in life, and this lack of trust keeps you out of the flow. The ego isn't in touch with life, so how can it trust it? When you are identified with the ego, you are fearful, confused, and distrustful. You don't know what to do. You look to the mind for answers, but its answers are jumbled and contradictory, and that leaves you all the more confused and distrustful. Until you know essence, you can't trust life because the ego *is* untrustworthy. Of course you can't trust life if you are trusting the ego's version of it. Essence is trustworthy, however, because essence is life—it is you disguised temporarily as a human being.

You can't know yourself as other than a human being while you are entrenched in the egoic state of consciousness. The egoic programming tells you that you are a man or a woman, which is decidedly human. You don't think to question this. Even religions don't lead you to believe otherwise. They describe a God, but this God is out there, not within you. The esoteric side of many religions does recognize the divinity within, however; so the truth is alive, even though buried. This basic lack of understanding about who you are, which is perpetuated by the egoic state of consciousness, is another block to being in the flow. *If you don't even know that you exist as essence, you won't look for it, and you won't know what it is when you do experience it.*

The egoic mind doesn't notice essence because it is too busy noticing other things. It focuses on things, sensations, feelings, desires, thoughts, the past, and the future. If all it did was focus on these, it wouldn't be a problem—you would land right in essence—but it doesn't stop at focusing. It takes an aspect of experience—a thing, a sensation, a feeling, a desire, or a thought—and spins a story about it.

Things, sensations, feelings, desires, and thoughts all come out of the moment and, by themselves, don't keep you from being in the flow. It is your relationship to them that can. The egoic mind's relationship to them is to judge them, evaluate them, resist them, deny them, try to change them, or tell a story about them. That is what takes you out of the flow. The antidote is easy—don't indulge in these mental tendencies. Just experience what is happening. Say yes to whatever is happening and just let it be the way it is.

Other people's egos also block the flow in the same ways that yours does. You need others to help bring about your plan, and you are needed to help bring about theirs. If others are not in the flow and not tuned in to their plans and yours, they won't be of much help. That is why it is important not only for you to wake up but also for others to wake up. Besides, everyone is part of a larger plan that serves all of humanity and this beloved planet. Fulfilling your plan contributes not only to your personal evolution but to the advancement of humanity.

In addition to egos interfering with the direction of the flow, circumstances created by them may be counter to it, and these may need to be changed before the flow can move as intended. The flow can get temporarily or permanently sidetracked by choices that are out of alignment with it. When that happens, essence may need to introduce an event to alter the circumstances and make room for new choices.

You have undoubtedly experienced this, either in minor or more dramatic ways: Something unexpected, shocking, or disruptive happens that causes you to see things differently and make different choices. It is usually a loss of some sort. It could be an illness, a divorce, a death, the loss of a job, physical incapacitation, the loss or destruction of a home, or the loss of savings. Any one of these events could cause you to restructure your life, and that restructuring is an opportunity for essence to have more say in your choices.

Such difficult experiences open people's minds to new possibilities and new ways of looking at things. During crises, insights and intuitions from essence and from others acting as mouthpieces for essence are more readily received. Difficult experiences undermine the egoic mind's power. They are humbling, as you face the fact that you (the ego) are not able to control life or ward off such things. In the midst of this humbling, essence is more easily experienced. You surrender to what is because there is no other choice. You are powerless to change the situation, so you accept it, and in that acceptance, lies the flow. During times of great duress, many report experiencing a power within them that sustained them, which they didn't know was there. That is essence. That is the gift in adversity.

Anything that dulls your awareness can also keep you out of the flow. Alcohol is a prime example, but extensive TV watching and other escapist activities, even immersion in books, can keep you from being aware of intuitions, insights, inspiration, wisdom, new ideas, guidance, and creativity, which may be coming out of the flow. These are just some of the things that come out of the flow. These also direct the flow, and if you miss them, you might miss where the flow is trying to take you. If you do, you will miss out on something more fulfilling than watching TV, drinking alcohol, or reading a novel.

CHAPTER 6
Co-creating with the Flow

Choosing by Deciding

When you make a choice, sometimes it is spontaneous and not thought about, like when you jump out of bed in the morning, and sometimes the options are laid out, examined, and decided on. These are two different experiences of choosing—one just happens and one is a decision.

Decisions always come from the mind. A decision is the result of making up your mind (an interesting turn of phrase). To the egoic mind, questions feel like problems that need to be solved by making a decision. There is a feeling of needing to make a decision, and almost any decision will do. To the egoic mind, making a decision is important because that ends the discomfort of not knowing. You make up your mind. You make it up!

The egoic mind wants to know, and it wants to know now. It has no patience with not knowing. Its job is to know, even if it doesn't, even if it is impossible to ever know. It is determined to know, to decide, and to give answers. Its very existence depends on knowing because if you stop turning to it for answers, it can't thrive. If you catch on that it doesn't know the answers to most of your questions, it is doomed. So it fakes it.

To the egoic mind, there is no sense of there being a right time to make a decision. To it, the right time is always now. It needs to know now. It makes you feel that it is wrong to even have a question, so it needs to make questions go away as soon as possible. It seems wrong to not know. How can you not know where to live, what you want to do for a living, what to eat for dinner, where to go on vacation? In the egoic state of consciousness, not knowing produces shame, and the longer you don't know, the more incompetent or inadequate you feel.

Because of this urgency to know, the egoic mind has developed many strategies for knowing. Asking others is a primary one: What do *you* think? You just go with someone else's answer. Research can be a variation on this: You research what others have chosen and what they have to say about that choice. This strategy appears less risky and more intelligent than just asking someone else. Then there is more serious research: You study the subject and draw conclusions from that. You list the pros and cons and then decide. The mind uses information to make decisions.

This way of making decisions has its place. It depends on what kind of question you are asking. If you are trying to decide on what kind of flowers to send your aunt, then it may be helpful to ask your cousin what your aunt likes best. Or if you need flowers that will last especially long for a bouquet you are putting together, research will give you the answer. However, other questions are not as suitable: Do I send flowers to my sick aunt or do I go visit her? How are questions like these answered? How do you decide something as simple as this? And what about the bigger questions: Who and when to marry, whether and when to have children, what career, where to live?

The egoic mind pretends to have answers even to these bigger questions. If you ask it, it will give you an answer or at least tell you how to find one. In the egoic state of consciousness, you turn to the mind for answers because you may not recognize any other possibility. It seems like *you* are the one running your life, so *you* must choose.

Since you see yourself as the one who is thinking, you assume your thoughts are what you think, so you do what you think. The egoic mind tells you to do something (because it is consistent with your conditioning and identity), and you do it. You don't even think to question it because you are programmed not to: That is what you think. End of story. In the egoic state of consciousness, the answer is whatever you think it is, and if someone disagrees, you argue your position because it's what *you* think.

You are identified with your thoughts in a way that causes you to believe them. This puts you at odds with others who are identified with theirs, which are different from yours. Are your thoughts better than theirs or are they just thoughts put there to make you unique and bring about certain lessons and actions? Your programming causes you to make certain choices, and those choices create your life—until they don't any longer. Your life is dominated and shaped by the choices you make from the egoic state of consciousness until you begin to wake up out of the trance created by your programming.

Knowing all of a Sudden

Something else is co-creating your life along with the egoic mind. It allows the egoic mind to have the influence it does, but all along it is offering other choices, other possibilities, than what the mind is offering. You are free to follow what you think or to follow these other possibilities. They are not immediately obvious, however, because they are not usually introduced through the mind but arise in the moment.

The greatest interference to becoming aware of these other possibilities is making another choice too quickly. The impatience of the egoic mind results in quick decisions, which often take you somewhere other than where essence would take you. *To discover where essence wants you to go, you often have to wait for the answer to arise in its own time.*

When it is time, the answer arises spontaneously out of the moment, and you often act on it just as spontaneously. When knowing does finally happen, it happens all of a sudden, but it may take days, weeks, months, even years to get to that point.

Knowing shows up all of a sudden, but you can't predict when that will be. You just have to wait for it, and the egoic mind doesn't want to wait.

When this sudden knowing happens, you know it because of how it feels. There is a sense of relaxation, relief, peace, elation—a yes—about a choice. Gone is all confusion, resistance, and doubt about what to do. It is clear and obvious. You know. This knowing feels solid, real, and unshakable.

When a decision is made from the egoic state of consciousness, the experience is a very different one. There is not the same relief, relaxation, or peace about it. The mind usually continues to think about it: "Did I make the right decision? What if …? Maybe I should …." It has decided, but this doesn't end the deliberation. This lack of peace is a sign that a decision was made by the mind. *In the flow, decisions arise—they are not made—and they stick,* while in the egoic state of consciousness, they are frequently changed.

There is a big difference between thinking and then deciding, and not knowing and then suddenly knowing. The difference is that no thinking is involved. That is a big difference. It might be hard to imagine life without deciding, but it goes much better than deciding before it is time to decide.

There is a reason for the timing of this sudden knowing. There is wisdom behind providing clarity when it is provided and no sooner. You learn to trust the wisdom of the moment— of the flow. Rather than "pushing the river" by choosing before it is time to choose, you wait and listen and trust that you will know when it is time to know, and no sooner. Essence operates on a need to know basis: You will know when you need to know and not before.

You learn to trust this. You can relax. All is well. When you allow it to, your life will be lived by the real you—by essence. The ego is out of a job. It still has a place, but now it is put in its place. It is not what it pretended to be, and it doesn't get to be that anymore. The rewards are great for this discovery:

peace at last, happiness—and fulfillment because the flow knows where it is going. It has always had a purpose. Now you can better align with that, and that will make you much happier than anything the ego could have created for you.

Why Decisions Can't Make You Happy

Decisions made by the egoic mind never lead to true happiness. At best, they lead to achievements, employment, prestige, power, knowledge, authority, money, success, praise, fun, excitement, experiences, pleasure, or friends, but none of these will bring you true happiness. Once you get them, you will want more or something else. They don't bring you the kind of peace and contentment that is the true measure of happiness.

But maybe that isn't what you want. There is a time for everything, and there is a time for wanting these things, even if they don't satisfy. There is a place for them in the drama of life. They are part of it and, in part, what you came into life to experience.

Good decisions lead to some measure of happiness, and part of this journey is learning to make good decisions. Good decisions bring rewards and bad ones don't, so you learn. This is what the world of the ego is all about—learning by choosing. However, this isn't the sole reason you came here. You are also here to be happy, to experience your true nature—essence—in the midst of the experiences you are creating.

It is obvious how bad decisions lead to unhappiness but less obvious why good decisions don't lead to real happiness. The main reason is that the ego's goals and the basis for its decisions are essentially selfish. The ego is motivated by a desire for power, greed, superiority, pleasure, control, safety, security, knowledge, praise—and yes—love, although it wants to be loved more than it wants to love. Since the ego can never have enough of these, no matter how much it has (more is always better), it will always be seeking and forever unsatisfied. The ego's fate is a state of dissatisfaction, which is punctuated only briefly by contentment.

As long as even good decisions are motivated by selfish reasons, it is impossible to be truly happy, because selfishness is alien to essence. It is not a quality of essence—quite the opposite. Essence is the experience of unity with all—with the experience that you are That, not separate from it. When selfishness and self-centeredness rule behavior, that behavior— no matter how positive it is in terms of worldly values—will not satisfy. Selfishness and self-centeredness keep you tied into the egoic state of consciousness, and that is an unhappy state.

Even in the egoic state of consciousness, there are tastes of happiness and peace, but these are like a drug to an addict because they are never enough. They cause you to pursue the thing that seems responsible for the happiness or peace. If you felt happy when you brought that new car home, maybe another one would make you happy again, or happier. Or maybe if you buy something else, at least it could bring you that feeling briefly. In the egoic state of consciousness, you are willing to settle for even brief experiences of happiness and peace because you don't know any other way to get these feelings. When you are deeply entrenched in the egoic state of consciousness, happiness and peace are hard to come by.

Another Way of Choosing

The only way out of this is to see that there is another kind of peace and happiness that is not dependent on doing or getting but on being. In the egoic state of consciousness, you are too busy to discover this. The egoic mind keeps you very busy doing and getting, and thinking about doing and getting. When you are preoccupied mentally and physically, you overlook what is actually living you—essence—and the joy it has in having this opportunity to be alive in a physical body.

Exercise: Witnessing

What is this that is aware of the whole game, of the *you* that you think you are, of all the doing and the getting? What is it that is witnessing this life *you* are presumably creating and living? What if that awareness—that witnessing—is who you really are, and it is just playing a game of pretending to be someone who is having a life? What would that feel like? How would that affect what you choose to do? If you didn't take yourself and your life so seriously, what would that be like? You would still be living this life and making choices, but it might feel more like a game, like something you could enjoy. You might actually feel like you have more choices. What would you choose then?

To discover what essence is choosing for this you that you think you are, you will have to be quiet and listen. This will bring you into the moment and into the flow, where the choosing is happening and has been happening all along. What essence chooses adapts to what you end up creating from the egoic level. It chooses alongside the ego and tries to carry out its plan and goals for this lifetime. The more time you spend in the flow, however, the more your actions and choices reflect the intentions of essence.

Essence will create quite a different life than the ego, although many things will be similar. Essence will express the same talents the ego did, but it will do it more skillfully, fluidly, and powerfully. Essence will express itself through the same personality the ego did, but it will do it more positively, without selfishness. Essence will still be faced with the challenges and karma of your particular body/mind, but it will handle them more gracefully and turn them into strengths. Essence may continue to make many of the same choices that your ego made. It may choose to remain in the same relationships, the same job, and the same location—or not. The shift from ego to essence may or may not result in changes in the structures of your life, but whatever changes are made will be more satisfying and fulfilling.

Certain things about your life are bound to drop away when you begin to allow essence to choose more, but it will be worth it. Once you experience what it is like to live from essence rather than from the ego, there is really no going back. You can't go back to the limited view and suffering of the ego. Why would you? The only reason you lived in the egoic state of consciousness was because you didn't know how to live any other way.

The return to essence is what your evolution has been about. You are here to express your particular flavor of essence in the world—to express essence through your particular talents and personality. No one has ever expressed essence in this way. *You are a completely unique expression of essence, and this expression will never come again through anyone else. Your uniqueness is deeply loved and appreciated by the Source.*

The best way to describe the experience of essence choosing is to say that it just happens. It doesn't feel much like a choice, which involves thinking and implies deciding between options. Essence chooses when you are not thinking. It chooses in between your thoughts. The choice pops into your mind or is expressed spontaneously through action, but you didn't arrive at it through thinking. When essence chooses, you know because the choice appears in your mind or body, and usually (hopefully) you don't spend time mulling it over. It seems obvious and right, and that is that. The experience is so different from choosing from the level of the ego that it is very easy to recognize once you see it as a valid way of choosing.

The egoic mind will tell you that you need to think about the choices essence makes. It will doubt them and try to confuse you with more thoughts, if you let it, because it doesn't want to be out of a job. Its job is to think and decide, and this is all it knows how to do. It doesn't trust any other way of doing things, and when you are identified with the egoic mind, either do you. However, when you have had enough experiences of essence choosing and the fulfillment that comes from that, you begin to trust it and allow it to happen more and more.

Allowing is the key to being aligned with essence and in the flow. Allowing requires receptivity rather than reactivity, which belongs to the ego. The ego is always reacting to life— taking action. When you are in the flow, allowing precedes action. You allow motivation, insight, ideas, and inspiration to arise—and then you act on them. In the egoic state of consciousness, these impetuses for action from essence are largely ignored. Instead, the ego makes up a reason for action and acts.

When you are in the flow, you move back and forth between being receptive and being active. Your actions are based on the motivation and ideas that arise out of the moment, which are not related to thought. *Thought might be helpful in implementing the action at some point, but it is not the source or reason for the action.*

There is an ease about actions that are rooted in essence because they are uncomplicated by the confusion of the egoic mind. When you are simply acting and not questioning that action or trying to manipulate life with it, actions feel clean (free of ego), clear, and fulfilling.

Actions that come from essence, regardless of what they are, are also innately fulfilling because they contribute to fulfilling the purpose of your life, and there is an inherent joy in doing that. Even very simple, ordinary actions can bring great joy and satisfaction when they are in service to essence and the reason you came into this life.

You don't have to be in the flow constantly for the flow to make a difference in your life. By meditating, just being quiet, or doing other enjoyable things that bring you into essence for a little while every day (e.g., hiking, running, biking, gardening, dancing, singing, painting, journaling, or playing or listening to music), you invite essence to co-create with you.

You will receive the insights and instructions you need to live much more peacefully and happily, even if you spend much of the rest of your time identified with the ego.

Co-creating with Essence

Insights received while spending time in the flow will improve your life immeasurably. Every insight and urge for action you follow reinforces your relationship with essence and trains you to be more in the flow. The more you say yes to the flow, the more prominent essence becomes in your life. You start wanting to be in the flow and not wanting to be anywhere else. That is when you really start paying attention to what brings you into the flow and what takes you out of it.

Initially, you may have to use your will to overcome the habit (and programming) of the egoic state of consciousness and do the things that bring you into the flow. Thinking is a habit, which can be replaced by a new habit—listening. You can't really not think because you can't control what arises in your mind. Even those who are awake have thoughts arise, but they have learned to not identify with them. Instead, they are identified with what is aware of the mind. What you can do is *replace thinking with awareness of thinking and with receptivity—listening. When you are identified with Awareness (essence) rather than with the egoic mind, it is a place of witnessing and allowing. You can arrive at this place by listening, or putting yourself in a receptive state.*

There is no getting around the need to choose essence over ego. This is a critical juncture in your spiritual life. *You can't become free of the egoic state of consciousness without making the choice over and over again to not identify with the ego.* No one wakes up without making this choice many, many times. When you have made it so many times that you spend more time identified with essence than with the ego, your identity will permanently shift to essence, and you will spend most of your time in the flow.

The amount of time you spend aligned with essence compared to ego determines how soon this shift will take place. That is why meditation and other activities that shift you into essence are so important and valuable. Those who awaken are invariably those who have had a steady practice of meditation or, through some other means, have spent a significant proportion of their time aligned with essence. They know what essence feels like, and this creates a desire for it. This desire is crucial for awakening.

Where does this desire come from? For that matter, where does the desire to meditate come from? Indeed, where does the desire to say no to your programming and no to the pleasure of indulging in the ego's tendencies come from? Of course, it comes from essence. When you are identified with the ego, you don't desire liberation from ego-identification and all that comes with that. *When it is time for you to awaken, the desire to awaken and all the desires leading up to that, such as the desire to meditate, come from essence. In a sense, there is another you that instigates the awakening process and begins to take over your consciousness, and that is the you that chooses essence over ego. When the time is right, essence incarnates and chooses itself.*

Whenever you choose to meditate or you choose essence over ego, essence is choosing this. What else could be doing this? Essence begins to wake up in this body/mind of yours, and it finds ways to keep waking up until it is fully incarnated. This can take quite a while. You (the ego) can fight it all the way, but essence will have its way with you eventually. The you that you now know yourself as will disappear, and in its place will be a new you, although with the same body, mind, conditioning, personality, talents, and karma. That you is essence incarnate.

Essence has always been active in your life as a co-creator. When you are identified with the ego, it co-creates with that. It allows the ego to create what it will and incorporates its plan into that. It breaks through the egoic state of consciousness regularly with its insights, wisdom, and impulses. It is by no means absent from this state and is still able to guide and influence your choices to some extent. However, once you are more aware of the flow and begin choosing essence over the ego regularly, your life becomes a happy and fulfilling co-creation, one in which essence predominates and you say "yes, thank you" to it all.

CHAPTER 7
Finding the Flow

The Tyranny of the Egoic Mind

The flow is not something you have to find as much as allow. The way you find the flow is by allowing. What you allow is whatever is happening. *It is happening, so just allow it to be the way it already is.* Besides, what is the alternative if that is what's happening?

The egoic mind offers other alternatives: denying, arguing with, or ignoring the flow. This is what creates suffering rather than what is actually happening, although you will never convince the mind of that. The egoic mind takes the fun out of life. It is the spoiler of every experience. It is a whiner, complainer, judge, critic, know-it-all, and tyrant. It is jealous, envious, and spiteful. It is just plain mean, and that just isn't fun to be with, for you or anyone else.

The egoic mind is the only thing that opposes what is. It makes no sense to do that, but that doesn't matter. It denies and argues with what is with "should nots": "This should not be happening," which translates to "This is not happening" and "This is not acceptable," as if this position has the power to change what is. The ego tries to convince you that if you don't like what is happening, you have a choice about it, when really your only choice is to deny it, argue with it, or ignore it.

The egoic mind ignores what is happening by replacing the *experience* of the moment with *thoughts*, either about what is happening or about something entirely different. It really likes thinking about the past and the future, and prefers those thoughts over ones about the present. If it thinks about the present, it is usually judging it, complaining about it, or arguing with it: "These dishes are so gross. I hate having to do them. Why do I always have to do them?" Judging, complaining, and arguing don't change the fact that dishes need to be done, and energy and attention are diverted into that rather than discovering how essence might experience dishwashing and when it might choose to do them. Perhaps this isn't the right moment to do them, but the egoic mind doesn't consider that.

The egoic mind intensifies the resistance to the moment by pushing you with "shoulds": "You should do the dishes now. You should do them this way. You can't ask your husband to help because men don't do dishes." And while you are doing them, it talks to you as if you were an incompetent child: "Don't forget to buy more dish soap. Don't be so sloppy with the water. Hurry up—you're missing your television show." The egoic mind is a nasty tyrant, and it can make even an enjoyable activity unenjoyable.

Not only does the egoic mind keep you out of the peace and contentment of the present moment with its thoughts, these thoughts often create negative feelings, pressure, and stress. The egoic mind tells you when to do something, how to do it, and what you are doing wrong. It is always reminding you of time and hurrying you up. It can be extremely bossy, unkind, and unforgiving. The worst atrocities on this planet have been carried out by those dominated by a very negative, tyrannical egoic mind. *While even pleasant thoughts can take you out of the beauty of the moment, negative thoughts make being out of the moment especially painful.*

Freeing Yourself from Identification and Negativity

Not all egoic minds are that tyrannical and unkind. As you evolve, you gain some mastery over the negative mind, and your thoughts become more positive and helpful. This evolution can happen within one lifetime or over many. Now, more than ever, through therapy and other means, overcoming the egoic mind's negativity is possible.

As a result, *many are getting free of their negative minds, mostly by learning to replace negative thoughts with positive ones. This is a big step toward freedom from the tyranny of the egoic mind, whose negativity and fear keep you tied to it. Detaching from a negative mind is difficult because thoughts feel very compelling when they are tinged with fear. Positive thoughts, on the other hand, can return you to essence because they reflect qualities of essence.* However, they usually aren't what is most present in the mind until much of the mind's negativity has been seen through and overcome, which can take some doing.

Ideally, thoughts would arise in your mind and you would recognize them as thoughts arising, and that would be that— you would not identify with them. Most thoughts don't deserve your attention. You can let them arise and let them dissolve. You won't miss anything you need to think because necessary thoughts and those from essence have a cleanness and feel about them that make them easy to distinguish from egoic programming. However, some thoughts are stickier than others—they hook you into paying attention to them. Thoughts that are negative or contain *I* are particularly sticky and the most likely to cause identification.

Nearly all thoughts from the ego, which are the ones you don't need to pay attention to, relate to the *I* and begin with *I*. *Most thoughts that relate to I are not worth paying attention to.*

Exercise: Busting the *I*

Notice how often thoughts that begin with *I* arise in your mind. What if all of these except the few functional ones (e.g., "I'm going to the bank") were ignored? Imagine what it would be like if you never again spoke any nonfunctional sentences that begin with *I.* How often would you say *I want, I like, I am, I will, I think, I have, I don't like, I don't want, I don't think, I don't have?* Watch the mind as it spins the story of *you* at every opportunity.

Seeing the strength of the I and not strengthening it by not identifying with it or giving it a voice is a very powerful spiritual practice. And it does take practice before dis-identification from the ego is more your usual state than identification. You have to see the story spun by the egoic mind again and again before you begin to see yourself as that which is aware of the story, rather than the storyteller.

Once you have achieved some dis-identification with *I,* not being hooked by fears and negativity arising in the mind is much easier. However, this is a Catch 22 because dis-identification from a fearful and negative mind is difficult. So, for most, the first step in the process of dis-identification is creating a more positive mind.

Did you realize that you have the power to create a more positive mind? You can use the mind to reprogram itself more positively. *Although you can't control what thoughts arise and you can't get rid of a thought once it is there, you do have the power to input new, more positive thoughts. These can neutralize those you can't control. This works because your mind works much like a computer.*

For a deeply entrenched thought, a lot of repetition and consistency will be necessary because you have been reinforcing it for so long by thinking it. To neutralize it, you will have to counteract it with a positive thought every time it comes up for some time. This gets easier over time because it will come up less and feel weaker when it does. These efforts are worthwhile and a very necessary part of waking up out of ego-identification.

The positive thoughts that will be most effective are ones that you believe. They must ring true for you. For instance, if the negative thought is "I have to make a lot of money for someone to love me," counteracting it with "I don't have to make a lot of money for someone to love me" will probably not be as effective as counteracting it with "People love me for my kindness and generosity," assuming that is true. Counteracting the negative with the opposite statement is less believable to the unconscious mind than counteracting it with a statement that is irrefutably true. Statements that ring the truest are likely to come from essence.

Exercise: Becoming Aware of Negativity

The first step in becoming free of negativity is becoming aware of the extent to which it is present. Observe the mind, like a curious scientist. What is it up to? Why those thoughts? What is it trying to do? Once you look, its motives are pretty transparent.

Most thoughts, especially *I* thoughts, are designed to support the current self image and keep you identified with that rather than with who you really are. To this end, the egoic mind will try to frighten you, build you up, or tear you down. It will do whatever it feels will be most effective in drawing your attention to the false you because once you pay attention to it, you become identified with it: Attention equals identification.

Notice how your thoughts are mostly about this *you*. In an attempt to perpetuate this *you* and inflate or deflate it, the egoic mind is forever comparing this *you* to others, checking to see how it measures up. Many of your thoughts are evaluative and judgmental because that is how the self image is maintained. *The egoic mind's job is to maintain the sense that you exist as a separate entity, and most thoughts serve this end; hence, all the thoughts about I. The mental world is a world of me, me, me.* You have undoubtedly noticed.

Negative thoughts, in particular, serve this end by getting you involved in trying to fix or improve something for this I. Negative thoughts generate feelings, which generate activity. They become the reason for taking action and end up structuring your life. They keep the story rolling along. Negative thoughts are particularly effective in maintaining the sense of *I* because you get hooked into believing that the egoic mind will save you from trouble, problems, and difficulties if you listen to it. What you might not realize is that the egoic mind created the problem in the first place simply by defining something as a problem. This gives it something to do and a reason for existing.

A simple example of this would be the belief: "I have to get this done before I go on vacation or I won't get a raise." This gets you very involved in planning how you will get it done, wondering if you will, being afraid of not getting it done, and thinking about what will happen if you don't and what has happened when you didn't. You have a real problem on your hands. The ego then tries to help you by giving you advice, pushing you, admonishing you, and scaring you. It creates an artificial goal and then makes this goal more important than it actually is. This gives the egoic mind a sense of being more important than it really is. This gives it—and *you*—lots to do.

Another example, using a more long-standing negative belief, would be: "I'm not good at making friends." This negative belief, like most negative beliefs, can be a self-fulfilling prophecy: If you believe this, you will probably not try to make friends, and your self image will be reinforced. Instead of being true, most negative beliefs actually create the situation they describe. This is why it is said that you create your reality. Your beliefs determine your experience, and your experience reinforces your beliefs.

Once you realize this is what the egoic mind is up to, you can choose to listen to its version of you and of life or not. Before this, the tendency was to accept its version as true, or at least to accept it as your version of things. Now you see that it is only a story, just one of many possible stories in fact. It has nothing to do with the real you.

Once you realize this, the negative voice of the egoic mind doesn't go away, obviously. It may even intensify, but you are now in a position to counteract it with another, more positive version of reality. Doing this is more effective than just disagreeing with the negative story (e.g., "I am good at making friends").

The most effective way to neutralize a negative story or belief is to reframe it. Reframing means that you tell the story in a more positive way. You tell it from the perspective of essence. This viewpoint isn't fabricated or untrue but more true. It is closer to the truth because it contains more of the truth of the situation. Negative beliefs frame a situation in a very tiny frame. They contain only a sliver of the truth, which results in a distortion—a lie.

To discover ways to reframe something, you might ask: What would essence say about this? Any answer that comes from essence will ring true and leave you feeling relaxed and at ease with yourself and with life. If you don't feel that way, you are still believing a lie.

For instance, in the last example, a reframing of the belief that you are not good at making friends might be: "Friendship is important to me, so I choose my friends carefully" or "My personality takes a while to relax around people." Either of these, assuming it is true, leaves you feeling accepting of what is, and that drops you into essence. In this way, a positive story—even though it is still a story—has the potential for being a bridge to essence. The egoic mind prefers a negative story because then it has a problem to think about and try to fix. Where are *you* if there is no problem?

The aspect of you that is able to bring in a more positive story is essence, which is always available to provide healing and show you the way out of the egoic state of consciousness. Therapists and friends often play this role as well. They have a more objective and compassionate view of you than you usually do. Those who have a very negative egoic mind due to abuse or trauma are most in need of outside help to overcome the tyrannical ego and support the development of a positive sense of self. This is done by learning to talk to yourself like a good parent rather than a tyrant. *Creating a positive, supportive, and kind ego is a big step in getting free from the ego altogether.*

Ask and You Shall Receive

Can't find the flow? Ask. Asking for help is a powerful tool in overcoming ego-identification and returning to essence. Asking can come in many different forms. Prayer is the usual way of summoning assistance of this kind. However, *your intentions and actions are also powerful statements of your desire to return to essence.* What you intend and what you do sends a message to unseen forces that you are ready to be helped.

Just as your prayers are heard and responded to by nonphysical helpers, so are your intentions and actions. Both are interpreted as calls for assistance. When you take a step toward essence, nonphysical helpers take many steps to assist you. However, they wait for you to choose this. As long as you choose the egoic state of consciousness, they work with you within this context the best they can. They do not push but patiently wait until you express a readiness and willingness to wake up from ego-identification. Once you show signs of this, they come forward and speed your awakening along. The more you ask for help, the more they help; and the more you do to be in the flow, the more they help you do that.

If you don't know this, you can't benefit from this as fully as you might. This is something you probably have to take on faith, but what is there to lose? *The egoic mind won't want you to believe in nonphysical helpers because this undermines its existence;* and yet, there is significant evidence for this, mostly from those who are able to see and hear them.

Essence, through nonphysical helpers, has always had ways of reaching people directly. Psychics and mediums have performed this role throughout the ages. Science is actually making it easier rather than harder to believe in the existence of life and activity outside the range of your senses. Why not? The Source has plenty of reasons for designing life this way.

Unseen forces help you in a number of ways. They help you realize essence, fulfill your life's purpose, and learn your lessons by speaking to you and others (who deliver messages to you) intuitively and in other ways. You feel an urge to do something, an idea pops into your mind, someone tells you something, a book winds up in your hands—all of these are ways unseen forces communicate with you on a regular basis. They serve essence by performing this function. This is their job, their life's work. You have yours and they have theirs.

These are the more obvious ways they guide you. They also are entrusted with arranging situations and bringing people together in ways that further everyone's plan. As you can imagine, this is a complex task, which requires constant supervision of the various activities people are engaged in. They do their best to shape the outcome of events, but sometimes things don't go as intended, and a new strategy is needed. Their work requires continually adjusting to people's choices and life as they are creating it.

Unseen helpers do this work in the present moment because that is where life is being carried out. If they are to have an impact, it is on what is happening now because the present moment is all there is. They work with whatever is arising right now, not with what arose yesterday or what will arise tomorrow because these are just figments of the mind. To take advantage of their help, you also have to be in the moment.

Fortunately, they are also able to interrupt the egoic mind with interjected thoughts, or many people would be difficult to reach. The intuition isn't well developed until later lifetimes, so unseen helpers often have to rely on other people who are receptive or intuitive to deliver messages to those they have difficulty reaching.

Other people are important for many other reasons as well. Besides being the context for many lessons, others are usually needed to fulfill the life purpose. Very few life purposes are accomplished alone. Most require many people, some who are familiar with each other and some who are not. When you ask for help from unseen forces, some of this help will come through others. The more you recognize this, the more likely you are to benefit from this and meet the people you need to fulfill your life's purpose.

Asking for help and acknowledging the existence of nonphysical helpers opens you up to realizing your connectedness with everything and experiencing this very personally. It becomes easier to see that others are yourself and that the One Source behind life is very wise and supportive. This makes it so much easier to relax, trust life, and enjoy the ride. The Source knows what it is doing.

How Good Habits Keep You out of the Flow

Even good habits can keep you out of the flow because they are based on "shoulds": "You should brush your teeth twice a day," so this becomes a habit. The problem is not so much with the habit itself if it is a good one, as with *when* and *how* you do it. Brushing your teeth twice a day is important, and establishing a time to do this daily helps you carry this out. However, time is part of the egoic mind's tyranny. It tells you when to do things and when to stop doing them. This timing is based on conditioning—ideas about when you should do things and for how long. This tyrannical relationship with time is what can cause even good habits to keep you out of the flow.

While you are carrying out a task that feels like a *should*, you are more likely to be present to your mental world than to what is. By capturing your attention with the issue of time, the egoic mind has you, and the path of least resistance is to keep listening to it rather than notice what else is present in the moment. The egoic mind involves you in how you should do whatever you are doing or it daydreams about something unrelated.

This can never bring you joy, only possibly some satisfaction in having obeyed orders. What can bring you joy in even the most mundane activities is being present to what else is arising in the moment in addition to your thoughts. Anything can be an enjoyable experience when you are really present to it. *What is the experience of this moment? What else is happening now? Those are the questions that can bring you into the flow and get you out from under the tyranny of the egoic mind.*

The flow has its own rhythm and timing, and it has nothing to do with clocks or shoulds. The knowing to do something arises and then it is done. Things that need to get done, including brushing your teeth, get done when you are in the flow. The flow is wise enough to take proper care of the body and to handle the responsibilities of life. You might even find yourself brushing your teeth for three minutes instead of two. What you will discover is that the resistance to doing this will be gone.

Living in the flow means allowing the flow to determine when you will do something. It might very well mean that you brush your teeth at the same time every day because essence is served by taking proper care of the body. Unless there is something else important to be done at that time, why wouldn't the flow take care of it at the usual time?

The difference between the egoic mind and the flow is that the flow is flexible and takes into account the freshness and newness of each moment and adjusts activity accordingly. The ego, on the other hand, demands that you do something at a certain time and in a certain way, which may actually go against the flow. *No wonder you feel resistance when you listen to the egoic mind: Not only is the ego's nature to resist, but what it says is often in conflict with essence.* In that case, resisting is good if what you are resisting is the ego. By all means resist unkindness, resist judgment, resist hatred, resist selfishness, resist false beliefs, resist the path of least resistance. Choosing to resist the ego's selfishness and bullying tactics will bring you into the flow.

The tyranny of the ego and its timetable is such that if you don't do something you "should" at a particular time (e.g., mail a birthday card on time), it scolds you, makes you feel guilty, scares you, or belittles you. This is how it keeps you on its timetable rather than in the flow.

This shaming and scolding often produces feelings, which strengthen the tie to the egoic mind because now you have feelings to deal with. Then the problem becomes what to do with these feelings and how to feel better: "Should I do this? What would Mom do? What happened last time I did that?" Or you might get involved in more self-talk: "So what. It doesn't really matter. Leave me alone." Even arguing with the egoic mind is still the egoic mind. You are stuck arguing one egoic position with another. If you had been in the flow, the experience would have been different: The flow would have sent that birthday card on time if it had been important or let it go if it was not. In any case, you would have been clear about your decision.

Action and non-action coming out of the flow is clean and clear, uncluttered by the confusion of the egoic mind, which contains so much contradictory conditioning. *The mind is no place to go for answers about how to live life.* It can help you find the address and put it on the envelope of the birthday card, but it isn't designed for much else.

The problem lies in not trusting the flow to do what needs to be done. Until you find out for yourself that the flow is trustworthy, the egoic mind will probably succeed in convincing you that it is not. Part of the problem in making the transition to being in the flow is that the egoic mind's idea of what needs to be done and the flow's are often very different. Many of the things that take up your time would not occupy you if you were living in the flow, or at least not as much. The egoic mind encourages you to do many things that do not enhance life but rather keep you tied to the suffering of its mental world. Nevertheless, changing your life in this way is a scary proposition—if you allow yourself to be scared by the ego.

How Bad Habits Keep You out of the Flow

Bad habits can be an even bigger problem than good ones when it comes to being in the flow. They become entrenched and difficult to break because they get tied to a mistaken belief, one that is usually laden with feelings. Furthermore, continuing a bad habit when it is known to be unhealthy creates more feelings, such as guilt, shame, anxiety, and fear, all of which keep you tied to the egoic state of consciousness.

Let's take the example of overeating, since it is such a common one. Overeating is driven by negative feelings, usually both repressed and conscious ones. Behind these feelings are negative (and false) beliefs, usually about yourself: I'm not lovable. I don't belong. I can't do anything right. I won't ever succeed. I don't ever get what I want. I won't be loved unless I succeed. I'm weak. I can't handle life. I'm a loser. I should be punished. I'm ugly. I'm a horrible person. These beliefs generate negative feelings, which in turn, reinforce a negative self image because if you are feeling angry, sad, anxious, depressed, guilty, fearful, ashamed, or jealous much of the time, you are not going to feel very good about yourself. The story of *you* is generated by these negative beliefs and feelings, and it is not a happy one. *You* become a really big problem to solve.

Because food is often tied to love, nurturing, kindness, reward, fun, happy times, and celebration, it is easy to imagine why someone who is unhappy might turn to food for a little happiness. Unfortunately, this only adds to the problem when indulged in to excess. Beliefs and memories around food are laden with positive feelings, and these keep you tied to eating as a route to happiness. You overlook all the ways overeating makes you unhappy—by feeling too full, gaining weight, and contributing to illness and a negative self image.

This narrow focus is the general state of the egoic mind. It overlooks so much of life, focusing only on what serves it. It doesn't notice the glistening pine needles or the shadows cast by the sunlight. What serves the egoic mind is the pattern of self-destructive activity generated by negative beliefs and feelings. Nothing is more effective in tying someone to the egoic state of consciousness than negative thoughts and feelings. The negative self image created by them and reinforced by a bad habit is the perfect environment for the egoic mind.

For one thing, it gives the egoic mind a problem to solve. When you are busy thinking and worrying about a problem, trying to solve it, and evaluating your progress, you don't notice what is actually happening in the moment. And if you aren't busy trying to solve the problem, you are so busy with the negative thoughts and feelings and engaging in the habit that you are not present to anything else. Your life becomes all about these thoughts, feelings, and actions, when it could be about so much else.

When you drop into essence, it is possible to see that your life doesn't need to be based on ideas and feelings about *you*. *You are not what you think you are. Stop paying attention to your thoughts and find out who you really are. When you stop paying attention to your thoughts, the stories and feelings and the activity driven by them stop. What a relief to find out there never was a problem.* Then you can discover what is arising out of the flow—what is true to do now, in this moment. That is all you need to know—what is true in this moment. *The other moments will take care of themselves. What about this one? What does it want? What is it about? Pay attention to now, and the rest will take care of itself.*

Habits that Can Bring You into the Flow

There are some habits that can actually bring you into the flow. They are habits that counteract your egoic programming. A habit is something you do again and again, which establishes it as an almost automatic, or at least familiar, behavior. To counteract the habit of identification with the egoic mind, you will need to practice being in the flow before it becomes your natural way of being. This may take a while because you have had so much practice going to your mind for answers. *Thinking is a bad habit.* So, now you need to develop some better habits, ones that will take you into the flow and help you stay there. Here are some suggestions:

1. *Make a habit of recognizing the egoic mind and not indulging it.* When a negative thought arises, don't believe it. See it as ego. When a complaint arises, don't speak it. See it as ego. When an unkind thought arises, don't speak it. See it as ego. When a judgment arises, see it as ego. When a comparison arises, see it as ego. When a story arises, see it as ego. Look for words like *always* and *never.* They are indicators of a story.

2. *Make a habit of noticing the I in your thoughts.* What follows is almost always ego. Don't indulge it. See it as ego and let it go.

3. *Make a habit of noticing your feelings.* Any thought that makes you feel bad comes from the egoic mind, not essence. Identify the mistaken assumption (belief) behind the feeling.

4. *Make a habit of noticing essence as it appears as Awareness.* Feel the energy of your true self. Notice how it has no location. When a thought arises, ask: Who is aware of this thought? When a feeling arises, ask: Who is aware of this feeling? When the *I* arises, ask: Who is aware of this *I?* These questions help you stay identified with essence as Awareness. Experience what it is experiencing.

5. *Make a habit of asking for assistance from unseen helpers.* Affirm your desire to be in the flow.

6. *Make a habit of doing things that return you to essence:* meditate, play music, sing, dance, create, garden, hike, etc.

7. *Make a habit of reading books that remind you about who you are.*

8. *Make a habit of spending time with those who are committed to living in the flow.*

9. *Make a habit of listening for guidance and acting on it.* This will develop your intuition and your connection to unseen helpers.

10. *Make a habit of saying yes to whatever is happening.* Be curious about whatever is arising. Stay alert and present to whatever is happening, without judging or evaluating it.

11. *Make a habit of expressing gratitude.* That will increase your ability to experience it. Gratitude is a sign that you are aligned with essence.

CHAPTER 8
Discovering the Direction of the Flow

Knowing and Not Knowing

It is nearly impossible to know where the flow will be going at some point in the future. It is only possible to see where it is now and where it is going from there. In any moment, the flow could change course dramatically. So many factors influence the direction of the flow that it is difficult to know exactly what will happen next.

In most moments, however, what happens next comes out of what just happened, so some prediction is possible based on this. The likelihood is that the next moment will come out of the circumstances of the last moment, except when it doesn't. Some moments are fairly predictable, but every moment is potentially a wild card.

The egoic mind doesn't like this, of course. It wants to know what is going to happen. It is actually more interested in what is going to happen than in what is happening because it is primarily concerned with safety, security, and survival and assumes that knowing what will happen will provide a better chance of achieving these goals. Because it feels the need to know, it tries very hard to, even though it is impossible. Even when it doesn't know, it takes a position of knowing because it would rather pretend to know than not know because not knowing makes it feel very vulnerable.

In the egoic state of consciousness, the drive to know and to be right is very strong. It is very apparent in conversations, which often entail intellectual sparing and fact sharing. The drive to know is so strong that people often say things they are not sure are true just to have something to say. They pretend to know something, and even fool themselves into thinking they know, when they don't. Even when they don't know something, they say it with great authority, as if saying it that way will make it so. The egoic mind doesn't really care if something is true or not, as long as others believe it is. The egoic mind is not into truth per se but being right, and it is up to doing whatever serves that end.

Exercise: Catching the Egoic Mind in Lies

Once you gain some dis-identification from the egoic mind, it becomes easier to see how often it comes up with lies just to look good. Most opinions are examples of this. Anytime you say "I think," watch what follows. Do you really know that to be true? When you examine a thought, you usually discover that you don't know whether it is true or not.

The egoic mind pretends to know about everything, and it has an opinion about everything. Notice how prevalent this know-it-all attitude is. Notice how important it is to the ego to be right, even on insignificant issues.

It turns out that knowing is not so easy. The truth is that you don't know way more often than you do. Seeing this helps you dis-identify with the egoic mind.

When you are very present in the moment, the experience is often one of not knowing. *An attitude of not knowing is the antidote to the certitude of the egoic mind, and it will bring you into the flow because it is more true: Most of the time, you don't know.* If you are going to take a position, the best position is that you don't know. This aligns you with essence, where a true and deeper knowing is possible, one that is relevant to the moment.

There are times when knowing is present, but it doesn't come from the mind. This true knowing comes from essence. When you experience it, it feels solid and real, yet humble and flexible. This knowing is a moment-to-moment knowing. Who knows what knowing will arise in the next moment? It may be very different. You don't know. All you can do is be very present to each moment and see what shows up.

Acknowledging that you don't know aligns you with essence because it allows for curiosity and acceptance, which are qualities of essence. It allows whatever *is* to be the way it is because you are not holding an opinion about it. When you take a position of not knowing, you are not thinking that whatever is should or should not be the way it is. You are just curious about it and very present to it, without presuming that it is right or wrong, good or bad. The position of not knowing even goes beyond that and presumes there is no right or wrong, good or bad. What is, is just what is. Why judge it? Who knows why it is? You are curious about what is, and therefore present to it, and let it be the way it is.

The egoic mind presumes to know what is right and wrong, and good and bad, but this is based on its beliefs and conditioning. It sees things narrowly. It can't see the bigger picture. It doesn't know what essence is up to. It doesn't know why things are the way they are. It just knows what it wants. It compares the moment to what it wants, and the moment almost always comes up short. You can't win when you are identified with the ego because it is never happy, and it doesn't know how to be happy.

Recognizing the Flow's Direction

There are ways to discover where the flow is going, at least momentarily. Within every moment are clues about the direction of the flow. What is arising now? Is the phone ringing? If so, the flow is going there. Is there an urge to sit down at your computer and write a friend? If so, the flow is going there. Is conditioning arising? That is the flow too. Whatever is arising in the moment is the flow. There are no mistakes: If it is arising, it is part of the flow.

The ego often disagrees with whatever is arising and tries to change the direction of the flow, then that becomes activity divorced from essence, and essence works with that in the next moment. In any moment, essence continues to offer its own possibilities for action, while the ego may choose other actions. In any moment, whatever is happening is being shaped either more or less by the ego or by essence.

Some things that arise from the moment are beyond your control and choosing (e.g., phone calls, urges, events, thoughts, feelings, desires, requests, insights), while others are choices (e.g., you choose to do something). Even the urge to choose comes out of the flow. When a choice needs to be made, the urge to make a choice arises. Some choices, however, come out of the egoic mind, not the flow.

The egoic mind often interferes with the flow by telling you that you need to make a choice, when that is not what is arising from the flow. If you listen to this, it throws you out of alignment with essence, and you are off and running in a different direction from that which essence intended. Essence allows these choices, and they become part of the next moment.

Meanwhile, the flow continues to bring phone calls, people, books, ideas, urges for action, urges to choose, intuitions, love, gratitude, and everything else you can imagine into your life. Life is happening, and it is rich with activity, creativity, love, abundance, and help from others if you make yourself available to notice these when they happen.

The way to discover where the flow is going is by observing what is coming out of it now, not by considering what came out of it in the past. The egoic mind bases its assumptions about the future on what happened in the past, but that is not really how it works. However, those beliefs can become a self-fulfilling prophecy. For example, if someone wasn't nice to you in the past, you assume she won't be nice now, and your attitude may evoke the coldness you expect. The past doesn't actually cause the future. There is only the present, and it arises fresh in each new moment. This is not how the egoic mind sees things though. Its job is to give meaning to events and experiences by spinning stories about them, which are largely based on what happened in the past and have at their core the belief in cause and effect.

Each moment has the seeds for the next, but you don't know how they will sprout or even if they will. Even when you are very present to the moment, you still can't really know what will happen. All you know is what *is* happening. Still, you can notice the seeds that are present. Each represents a potential direction for the flow.

Here is an example to illustrate the rich and unpredictable possibilities within each moment: Let's suppose that one of the things that is arising in the moment is the urge to pick up the phone and ask your friend to help you with a project. In the next moment, a thought arises about whether you should do that, and you ignore it and make the phone call. In the next moment, you discover that your friend is not home. That seed didn't sprout, but it might have. A possibility existed for that moment in time to become something other than it did, but it didn't. Now you respond to the urge to do something unrelated to the project, so you do that. While you are doing that, you realize how to complete the project without help, so you stop what you are doing and do that. Maybe you will complete it then or maybe you will be interrupted by another urge or something else. The project gets completed, and all of the time, you were in the flow.

Here's another scenario: You are working on a project, and you need some help with it. You don't respond to the urge to call your friend for help. Instead, you respond to your conditioning about not wanting to ask for help, and you don't call her. Then the thought arises: "You need to get this done now. Hurry up and figure this out." You decide this is true. Immediately your body responds by hurrying, and you begin to feel anxious and stressed. Then a daydream arises about what it would be like to be done. Then the mind suggests: "I need a break. Some ice cream would really taste good." You gladly take that suggestion, and this adds guilt to your anxiety, but you ignore these feelings and have a nice big bowl. Now you are not feeling so good. "I need a nap. I can figure this out later," you think. You take a nap. A couple of hours later, you feel ready to think about the project again: "How do I get this finished?" You think and think, but you can't come up with an answer. You have an urge to call another friend, and you do that. While you are complaining to her about your day, she makes a suggestion, and you realize how to complete your project. The project gets completed (thanks to a friend's intuition), and all the time, you were out of the flow.

Whether you are in the flow or out of it, life happens—but it happens differently. Sometimes, it doesn't end as nicely as this when you are out of the flow. Days can be taken up accomplishing something that might have taken only hours if you had been in the flow. Or worse: Something that was potentially fulfilling or necessary to your plan didn't happen because you didn't pick up on any of the clues the flow was giving you.

The flow has a way of communicating its direction to you, but you have to listen and be willing to follow its nudges, which usually come in the form of intuition and urges to act. It rarely speaks in words, except through other people, so you need to be in a receptive state to catch its communication.

However, that is impossible if you are thinking. *Thinking blocks the channel of communication between you and essence because you can't think and listen at the same time.* When that happens, essence has to find another way to communicate with you, perhaps through someone else, who hopefully is listening and willing to respond.

The danger of being strongly identified with your mind and thoughts is that you may miss the messages the flow is sending you about where your deepest fulfillment lies. The flow is trying to unfold your plan, and it can only do this if you are open to its ways of doing this. The egoic mind is not driven to help you fulfill your plan because it is driven by its own agenda, which can't bring you happiness because it is selfishly motivated and ignorant of the intentions of essence. *If you allow the egoic mind's choices to become yours, you are likely to create a very different life than what essence would create— and not nearly as happy and fulfilling.*

When you are deeply entrenched in the egoic state of consciousness, the ego rules your choices. This is why so many are miserable. Not only are they living a life that can't make them happy or fulfilled, but they are living with a tyrant at the helm, who is never satisfied with however life turns out.

Essence is not content to have you suffer. When you have lost your way, it intervenes to bring you back into the flow. It does this primarily through loss and crisis. Through illness or by removing something or by dissolving some of the structures you have created (e.g., job, partner, home), essence is often able to interrupt the egoic trance and bring in new possibilities more in line with the life you were meant to live. Crises have a way of bringing the ego to its knees and opening you up to new ways of looking at your life and to people who can help you rebuild your life more satisfactorily.

There also are many who live quite happily because, although identified at times with their egoic minds, they respond to the flow enough that their life purpose does get fulfilled. *To fulfill your life's purpose, you only need to be in the flow some of the time—just long enough to listen and respond to it.* As in the previous example, the intentions of the flow can often still be fulfilled even if you are not always in the flow, as long as you respond to the flow at least some of the time.

This is why daily meditation and other spiritual practices are so important. If you are spending a lot of time identified with the egoic mind, meditation breaks the egoic trance temporarily. It allows essence to break through and the flow to be communicated to you. When you are quiet and receptive, it finally has access to you, and if you listen and invite it, it will communicate what it needs to, to you. If you have a very busy mind, you may need to make room for this so that you don't lose your way.

The more you respond to the flow, the happier and easier your life will be. Because living in the flow is so rewarding, everyone eventually learns to be in the flow and stay there. When this happens, you graduate from this physical plane and go on to another to learn other lessons and accomplish other tasks.

Exercise: Noticing Where the Flow is Going

As you go about your day, notice what arises within you to do. Do you do those things right away as they arise, or do you think about them and decide to do something else? What is the basis for deciding to do something else? Usually it is a belief that stops you from spontaneously following an urge to do something. Notice what thoughts tend to sidetrack you from following these spontaneous urges arising from the flow.

These spontaneous urges should not be confused with desires. Desires also arise in the moment accompanied by an urge to fulfill them, but these urges are different from the urges that come from essence. Most desires and thoughts come from the egoic mind. It is best to just let them be there and then notice *what else is present now* because that will tell you more about what the flow intends than your thoughts or desires.

An urge to do something that comes from essence will feel different from an urge to do something that comes from the egoic mind, so pay attention to how an urge to do something feels. If it feels expansive, positive, solid, real, and true, then it is from essence. If it feels compulsive, contracted, fearful, petty, or negative, then it is from the egoic mind.

Tools for Understanding the Flow's Direction

There are also a few esoteric tools that offer a glimpse into the bigger picture, or plan, the Source has for you. Astrology, numerology, palmistry, and Tarot are the most common ones. These tools can give you a more general picture of the flow (the plan) over the course of a lifetime, although the Tarot's strength is more in describing the forces active in the moment.

The helpfulness of these tools is highly dependent on the ability and intuition of the person using them.

Astrology is the most comprehensive of these. The astrology chart is a picture of the heavens at the moment of birth. Everything born at that moment is a reflection of the energy of that moment, and this energy imprint can be read in the chart. Astrology is the closest thing to a science of psychology that exists. It provides a means for understanding your psychological makeup as well as your spiritual lessons and life purpose. Your chart describes your unique personality, or costume, for this lifetime, which is designed specifically for you to learn certain lessons and accomplish certain goals.

The soul (the aspect of the Source that reincarnates) chooses the moment of birth because it provides the imprinting, or programming, it needs to learn its lessons and fulfill the chosen life purpose. Before coming into life, you decide, with the help of your guides, what you will try to accomplish in the upcoming life. Then, the moment of birth is chosen to provide an energy imprint that will support these goals. There are many possible moments that could provide this.

No one knows if you will succeed in meeting these goals. Because you have free will, your life could go in a different direction. If that happens, you will learn and, hopefully, accomplish other things. Usually, however, the intended goals are met at least to some extent because the imprinting makes certain choices more likely than others. It is rare that anyone lives a life extremely different from that intended. When this does happen, it often results in illness, disease, mental illness, or depression. These may be signs that someone is not living the life he or she was meant to live, but not always. These also may be challenges that were freely chosen to provide growth.

Those who understand their programming, which includes psychological tendencies, needs, and drives, have a much better chance of overcoming their negative conditioning and making use of their talents. The success of psychotherapy attests to the value of psychological awareness and understanding. Awareness is the first step in overcoming conditioning that can interfere with fulfilling your potential and life purpose. If you don't see something as a problem, you won't apply yourself to overcoming it.

Astrology is able to pinpoint the conditioning that is likely to cause the most suffering. This understanding can be used to help you detach from it and not respond to it in detrimental ways. Astrology has the added value, which psychotherapy does not, of being able to describe your talents, how these talents might best be used, and what activities will bring you the most fulfillment. Psychotherapy has no concrete way of knowing these things, but must rely on the therapist's intuition and the client's subjective view of himself or herself.

Astrology offers something else that psychotherapy cannot: It provides a picture of where the flow is going now and its likely direction in the future. It gives insight into the unfolding of your life plan and the challenges you might meet along the way, which serve both to strengthen you and develop your talents. Astrology helps you see that even challenges are part of the flow. This makes it more likely that you will turn the lemons in your life into lemonade rather than feeling victimized or blaming others.

The Feeling of Being in the Flow

When you are in the flow, you know it. Being in the flow produces the feelings everyone wants to feel. In short, you feel happy. This happiness is not the happiness that comes from getting your way but from *finding your way.* When you are in the flow, you are aligned with essence—with who you really are. You have returned to essence, and that is what makes you happy. It is what this journey has all been about. When you experience that sense of being Home, it brings great relief, relaxation, and expansion of your Being. You feel all of the qualities of essence: peace, contentment, acceptance, clarity, wisdom, and joy. You feel elated to be Home.

Joy is a real sign that you are in the flow. It comes from the relaxation, relief, and ease you feel as a result of being free of the dominance of the egoic mind. Being identified with the egoic mind is very unpleasant, but you resigned yourself to this for a time because you didn't know what else was possible. Within everyone, however, is a sense that happiness is possible and a longing for it. When you actually discover that you were right—that it is possible to be happy—you feel elated.

The more the feeling of being in the flow happens, the more you say yes to it, and you begin living in the flow more and more. You learn to trust it, and it becomes your way of being in the world, and joy becomes your ongoing experience. That joy is the reward for waking up out of ego-identification. It isn't easy, but it is so worth it. Besides, it isn't really a choice. Suffering eventually drives you out of the egoic state of consciousness and back to essence, where you belong. What a joy to be alive, and what an amazing journey this is!

CHAPTER 9
How Life Comes out of the Flow

How Planning Keeps You out of the Flow

The egoic mind has difficulty seeing the flow in events because it is usually too busy planning for some future event or ruminating about the past. When the need to do something does arise out of the flow and the ego notices that, it takes it on as its personal mission. Using the past as a guide and other information it has gathered for how it will proceed, it creates a plan for action. It decides exactly how and when it will do it, not realizing that the flow already has a plan. The ego assumes a plan is needed and that providing it is its job.

At other times, the ego generates its own ideas about what to do, which may not be at all what essence intends, and follows those as if there is nothing else coming out of the flow. It ignores what is coming out of the flow and acts independent of it. The ego doesn't perceive that anything worthwhile is coming out of the flow. It discounts or disregards many of the insights, solutions, and urges to act that arise from essence. It assumes that it is the only player here, and it convinces you of this too.

It even seems this way because the flow's timing is not what the ego would like. The flow has its own timing, which is not revealed before it happens. The ego assumes it needs to take control of life because it often seems like nothing is happening, and it is very unhappy with that. Almost anything seems better than that. The ego is at odds with the natural ebb and flow of life, and it pushes and tries to make life conform to its schedule. It is impatient with life as it is.

The flow has a plan, which unlike the ego's, will bring you the life you are meant for, but you don't know what the specifics of that plan are until it is time for you to know. The good news is that you don't need to know before you do. The egoic mind wants to, of course, because knowing helps it feel safe, but you don't really need a plan. You just need to wait for the next step to be revealed. There is nothing you need to figure out, although the ego will not be convinced of this. *Your job is just to give your attention to what is and allow the flow to show you what it wants next from you.*

When you are in the flow, you are a responsive instrument of essence. You respond to the urges, inspiration, and knowing that come out of the flow. For this, you need minimal thinking. Far more important than thinking is listening because it puts you in a receptive state. *Listening brings you into the flow, while thinking takes you out of it.*

Being in the flow does not feel passive, however, but alive, exciting, responsive, and active. You enthusiastically move through your life, doing many of the same things you always have done, but with more joy and certainly more fulfillment. When you are in touch with essence, any activity is joyful. You do what is necessary to sustain yourself in the world, but you don't waste your energy on activities that aren't fulfilling.

When you are in the flow, your activities bring joy not only because you are present to them, but because they are aligned with essence and your life plan, and therefore intrinsically rewarding. Some of these activities might be considered by others to be ordinary or uninteresting, but because they are aligned with your life's purpose, they are rewarding and joyful to you. That is what it is like to be in the flow.

You already know what it is like to be out of the flow. Rather than being an instrument of essence, you are divorced from it and usually at war with it. Being out of the flow is effortful, difficult, and unpleasant. Nothing is ever good enough, and potentially wonderful moments are often tarnished with judgment, comparisons, discontent, fear, or depression. *When you are out of the flow, you get things done, but they don't bring much satisfaction or joy, both because you are not present to them and because they are not intrinsically satisfying. If what you are doing doesn't fit your plan, it won't satisfy you even if it would satisfy someone else.*

You can't be fulfilled by someone else's life purpose; you can only be fulfilled by yours. *You won't find out what your life purpose is by listening to the egoic mind because it doesn't know. Only by paying attention to what is coming out of the flow and letting that lead you through your life will you fulfill your life's purpose.* The egoic mind will lead you if you let it, but don't. You can trust the flow to unfold your life—more perfectly than you ever imagined. However, you won't know this until you give it that opportunity by paying attention to it.

Exercise: Noticing the Mind's Tendency to Make Lists

Making lists is one of the egoic mind's favorite activities. It is one of the primary ways it manages reality. It is not only part of planning any future event, but also part of planning daily activities. Notice how often during a day your mind recites its list for what it has planned for the day. It even goes over the steps necessary to complete each activity. During the day, it often evaluates its progress in accomplishing what it set out to do. It lists what it did and what it has left to do, how it went, and its concerns about how the rest will go and if everything will get done.

Notice how much this consumes your thoughts. Moreover, notice how this list-making creates a hurry-up mentality, one in which the sole objective is to get something done according to an arbitrary schedule, sometimes at the expense of other values, especially enjoyment. The egoic mind's drumbeat is "Hurry up and get it done!" This tendency to name and rename things you need to do in the future makes it seem like there is never enough time. It leaves you feeling stressed out, overwhelmed, and inadequate.

This list-making and hurry-up mentality saps the joy out of life because while you are doing it, you are not present to what you are doing, and you are missing out on the experience of essence in that moment. It seems like this is the way to get things done, but there is another way: Just listen and respond. Discover how beautifully essence brings about life.

How Planning Comes out of the Flow

Planning would not be such a problem if it didn't involve thinking because when you are planning, you are involved with the mind, and that usually means the egoic mind. The mind can be, and is, an instrument of essence as well as of the ego. However, in the egoic state of consciousness, your mind is the servant of the ego. Although the ego doesn't actually exist, it has an apparent existence. It is the programmed sense of being a separate entity, the feeling that you exist as *I*. When the mind is driven by the ego, most of your thoughts serve the ego, and many begin with *I*.

"I" thoughts still arise when you are awake and in the flow, but you no longer think of yourself as this I. You realize these thoughts are the conditioning that creates the ego. When you are in the flow, thinking still happens, but the mind becomes more of an instrument than a tyrant and serves more of a practical function. In seeing that you are not the egoic mind, it is much easier to not identify with conditioning when it arises. Your conditioning seems more like it doesn't belong to you, which is the truth.

Your conditioning never belonged to you. It is just part of the programming that created the ego, which was never you, although you were programmed to think it was. Now your conditioning can be met with the acceptance and compassion of essence. That means that you also meet other people's conditioning with more acceptance and compassion. Love, instead of fear, is your natural state when you live in the flow.

The mind functions more in the background when you are in the flow, and it is more possible for essence to communicate with you through thoughts than before. Thoughts from essence stand out in the mind, like color does next to black and white, or like something three-dimensional does next to something two-dimensional. Thoughts from essence are easy to recognize compared to the usual conditioned thoughts. They have an energy and aliveness to them. When you recognize them, you feel happy, excited, and expansive.

When essence uses the mind, it doesn't feel the same as when the ego does. When the ego thinks and plans, it is involved with I: I will do this, and then I will do this, and that will be good (for me). Planning is oriented toward getting what the ego wants. It involves a lengthy stream of thoughts, which are frequently returned to and can be obsessive. The thoughts often go in one direction and then another. The egoic mind is changeable and fickle when it is in planning mode. It is confused and uncertain, so it explores many possibilities and jumps from one to another.

When essence uses the mind, on the other hand, it doesn't result in planning as much as just doing. Essence inserts a phrase here and a phrase there when the time is right to do something. These phrases are more like gentle commands: "Do this now. Now do this. Okay that's enough. That's good." This is how the flow's thoughts come through, not in lists but in ideas to do something in the moment. When they register in the brain, they feel like a light bulb just went on. These thoughts have a kind tone, like that of a wise and good parent or teacher. They feel solid and unwavering, and you feel their truth. You feel loved and supported by this voice. As you evolve, this voice becomes stronger, more recognizable, and lengthier.

When you are in the flow, you may not even realize that what you are being spontaneously moved to do is part of a larger plan. You respond to an idea or urge that comes out of the flow, and it may only be later, when you see the results, that you realize the purpose of your actions. The ego, on the other hand, has an idea in mind of what it wants to achieve and plans accordingly. *The flow moves you, and you may not know what it is up to. A plan exists, but you are not necessarily privy to it.* This is why it seems to the ego that the flow doesn't have a plan.

So much time is wasted in the egoic state of consciousness in planning unnecessarily—or worse, in following plans that are ill-conceived and ill-timed. Seeing this is part of your evolution, and you do learn from your choices, so you are allowed to make them. The difficulties and suffering caused by not allowing life to flow cause you to wake up out of ego-identification. You eventually realize how ineffectual the ego is at running your life.

How Talking Comes out of the Flow

Most talking is unnecessary and serves the ego. Most is a direct and automatic expression of a thought that comes into your mind. When you are identified with your thoughts, you speak them without questioning or evaluating them. The ability to be aware of and evaluate your thoughts develops only as you evolve. This ability to be objective about your thoughts is essence breaking through into the egoic state of consciousness. This is a huge step in evolution because this objectivity makes it possible to become free of the egoic mind. Before that, essence broke through only occasionally and was often disregarded. As this evaluative function develops, essence becomes more available in your life.

Meditation is the most important thing you can do to strengthen this awareness and objectivity and the availability of essence. *Because meditation builds a bridge between the mind and essence, it takes you out of ego-identification and into identification with essence as Awareness. The more you experience essence as Awareness, the stronger your identification with it becomes. You have to travel this bridge many times, and then one day, you stay on the other side—in essence—and you don't come back, except possibly during brief bouts of re-identification with the ego.*

Most talking is the ego talking, not essence. You know essence when it speaks. The words from essence carry no judgment, comparisons, fear, or superiority. They feel good to both the speaker and receiver. Love, peace, contentment, relaxation, and a sigh of relief are all signs of essence speaking. When essence speaks, it speaks simply and straightforwardly. It goes right to the point. It is usually received without disagreement, with a quick and simple yes, and with gratitude.

You can often see and feel essence as well. When essence speaks through you, a power in your voice and eyes causes those listening to take note. You may also feel this power as warmth and energy, and you and others may also feel chills.

When your words come from essence, they seem to pop out of your mouth. You didn't think about saying them beforehand, and you didn't know you were going to say them. They may come as a surprise, but a pleasant one. Because they don't feel like they came from you, you don't feel like you can take credit for them. They feel like they came through you, which is the truth. This phenomenon is very common really, especially around those who offer themselves to essence.

You don't have to be living in the flow and fully identified with essence to speak these words. Anyone can be a mouthpiece for essence. However, the more intuitive you are, the more easily and commonly this happens. Some express essence much of the time. Often they are spiritual teachers, counselors, or healers, but they don't have to be. What matters is the extent to which someone is intuitive and has given himself or herself to essence.

Those who have developed their intuition to its fullest may act as direct channels for nonphysical helpers. However, be aware that channels have their lessons too and not all are created equal, free of ego, or able to tap into true helpers. They earn their ability to do this through dedication to essence and to their own personal evolution.

Imagine what it would be like if you only spoke when it served essence and you withheld all of the egoic mind's opinions, judgments, comparisons, and musings about the past and future. Imagine how this would affect your relationships. It would completely revolutionize your life. Where you now create enmity, hurt, jealousy, anger, and boredom with your words, you would create love, peace, acceptance, and happiness.

Imagine what would happen if this spread around the world. This is how peace and love enter this world—no other way, not through legislating, waging wars, redistributing wealth, or punishing people for misbehaving. Peace and love come into this world one person at a time through a change of consciousness. Since you can't change other people's consciousnesses except by changing your own, the task is simple: Wake up from the egoic trance. Refuse to identify with the egoic mind, and say yes to essence—your innate goodness.

One reason more people don't live like this is that they don't know it is possible. They are resigned to the human condition, the ego, and the meanness in themselves and others. They try to be kinder, but it is an uphill battle. Religions try to remedy this with rules and commandments, but these rules will not be followed until people realize that the egoic mind is not who they are and that it is possible to dis-identify with it and identify with something else. If you don't know this, it will be more difficult to do this. This kind of knowledge is power— real power—to transform yourself and the world.

You don't have to stop talking altogether except when essence is speaking through you. That would be very awkward in social situations. Sometimes essence doesn't have anything to say. In fact, that is more often the case than not. In addition to needing to communicate for functional reasons (e.g., "Please pass the butter"), you communicate to connect with others: to give support; to share experiences, insights, and information; and to express needs, feelings, and preferences. These can be very positive and enriching exchanges even though they may not be essence speaking.

Relationships depend on communication, and communication is made for relationships. Without someone to communicate to, you wouldn't even need to communicate. Understanding this—that communication is for supporting relationships—will help you define for yourself what kind of communication is in keeping with living in the flow and what is not. Some kinds of communication obviously take you out of the flow, particularly criticism, judgments, complaints, and other forms of negativity, because they are aligned with the ego, not essence.

Sharing stories about the past and dreams of the future with others can be useful. It is a way of determining how well you fit with someone. Learning about someone's past and someone's dreams tells you a lot about whether you might have something meaningful to share together. That kind of sharing of the past and future is functional. However, repetitive stories rarely serve a relationship nor does, for example, bringing up the past to criticize someone.

The guideline for speaking (in addition to functional communication) is, Does it enhance the relationship and the other person or undermine, tear down, or diminish? If what you want to say doesn't have the potential for affecting the relationship or the other person positively, then it serves no purpose to say it. If it is likely to have a negative effect, it is certainly best not to say it. Let it go. Your relationship will thank you.

You usually know if something is going to have a negative effect before you say it, but you may say it anyhow. Sometimes hurt is intended, but usually this is an attempt to get your way, change the other person, or reinforce your self image.

Judgments and criticism may seem justified because you think it is your duty to try to change others, presumably for the better. You think they should be different because of your conditioning, so you try to fix them for their own good and for the good of the relationship (but really for yourself). Getting someone to change is most people's idea of improving a relationship, but that doesn't work. *Criticism is the fastest way to kill love and cooperation.* The critic holds himself or herself superior, and relationships can't thrive in that climate. They thrive on mutual respect, cooperation, helpfulness, and kindness. If you want your relationships to work, then make others feel good, not bad. Making others feel bad is a recipe for bad relationships.

Making others feel good is an excellent goal in communicating with them. It is the antidote to the egoic mind, which tends to do the opposite. What you say can be as simple as complimenting their appearance or as profound as telling them what they mean to you. It's okay to make someone's ego feel good. Catering to someone's ego with kind words is better than catering to yours. However, it is more beneficial and rewarding to everyone to compliment and point out someone's goodness. *Saying something that makes others feel good, regardless of what it is, aligns you with essence, and if you are not already in the flow, it can put you there.* Try making this part of your spiritual practice. It will make you feel good too.

Exercise: Making Others Feel Good

The next time you are standing in line at the grocery store (or somewhere else), think of something kind and cheerful to say to the checker or someone in line. Don't draw attention to yourself while doing this by saying *I.* Start your sentence with *you,* and you will be off to a good start. See if you can continue speaking, without referring attention back to yourself with a story or an explanation of what you like, think, or do. Notice how good this feels. *Goodness is its own reward.*

When you are not saying something positive, listening to others is just as powerful a spiritual practice. This kind of listening is more of a listening with your Heart for the purpose of uncovering what someone might need in the moment. Essence will reply if it has something to say, but listening, itself, is a powerful support to others when you are present to them from essence.

Exercise: Being Present to Others

When you are with others, let your goal be to really see them and to be present to them in the moment, and let any speech come from there. Assume that you are there for them, not the other way around. To be there for them, you must be very present to them. Only from that place, can you serve them the way they need to be served.

Notice the tendency of the ego to want to interrupt and turn attention onto itself. Instead of indulging this tendency, be very present to what someone is saying, even if it doesn't interest you. Be present to his or her essence. Can you detect it? Even in speech that is laden with ego, essence is present behind the scenes. Try experiencing the essence of others while they are talking. In experiencing theirs, you will experience yours.

Giving, whether it is kind words or an ear, truly does feel better than receiving. *Moreover, giving your attention (awareness) to others rather than receiving it aligns you with essence and helps you avoid indulging in any egoic tendencies.*

Work and Play

Work and play are both concepts. They are creations of the mind. There is really only experience. Whether you call what you are experiencing work or play depends largely on your level of enjoyment. Enjoyable experiences are considered play, and unenjoyable ones are generally considered work. When you are living in the flow, these distinctions become irrelevant because experience just is what it is, and there is joy in whatever is. When you are in the flow, it is possible to in-joy (find joy in) any experience because joy is available in every moment.

This joy is often overshadowed by other aspects of an experience, especially thoughts about it, but also by strong sensations, such as pain, which are labeled undesirable by the egoic mind. Nevertheless, however subtle, joy is a quality of every moment. This joy is the Source's joy about being alive and having experience—any experience.

Essence relishes every experience, even unpleasant ones, because it knows that whatever is happening is momentary and fleeting. This is obviously true, but the egoic mind doesn't recognize the fleetingness of the moment or the impermanence of life and therefore fails to take this into account in assessing the moment. It focuses on what it doesn't like about the moment, as if it is a permanent condition, and becomes miserable over it. *Essence, on the other hand, is in touch with the impermanence and therefore preciousness of life. It relishes every moment, which is entirely unique and will never come again. This is how you, too, can experience life when you are in the flow.*

Once you begin living in the flow, concepts such as work and play do not have the meaning they do in the egoic state of consciousness. You still use these words to communicate, but the boundaries between work and play do not exist in your experience. When you are in the flow, every moment feels like play; while in the egoic state of consciousness, most moments feel more like work.

Play is a good way to describe the experience of living in the flow because it reflects the lightheartedness, ease, and acceptance of being aligned with essence. When you are in the flow, life feels easy, light, and a-okay. As in play, there is very little thinking going on, certainly not the kind that spoils your good time. If thinking is happening, it is either functional or upbeat and positive, kind and supportive. Being in the flow, like play, is a time when you feel free to express yourself and do what you feel moved to do.

This freedom comes from being free of judgments. When you are in the flow or playing, you are not involved in analysis, judgment, or opinions. Play is about having fun, and judgments and opinions are fun-stoppers. To be in the flow or to play, you have to be free of criticism, both of yourself and others.

When you play, you like what you are doing, so you say yes to it. This acceptance puts you in the moment (and in the flow) and allows fun to happen. Happiness comes forward in an atmosphere of acceptance, while it is squelched in an atmosphere of criticism.

When you are playing and having fun, humor naturally arises, as it does when you are in the flow. The kind of humor that arises from the flow is good-natured, kind, loving, embracing of life and others—not cutting and sarcastic, which is the ego's brand of humor. That kind of humor is designed to build the ego up by tearing others down. It is often cruel and at someone else's expense. It finds fault with life.

Humor that comes from essence, on the other hand, expresses enjoyment of life, especially of the differences between human beings. It pokes fun at the ego. It helps you laugh at your humanity in a way that allows you to both accept it and see it for what it is—not the whole story of who you are. After all, what is it that is able to enjoy your foibles and those of others, if not essence?

Essence is having great fun playing this game of hide and seek with itself. It takes great pleasure in unmasking the illusion of a separate self and pointing at the foolishness and inconsistencies of the egoic mind. This kind of humor can help people wake up because it comes from a place that is beyond the ego, one that is not caught up in the conditioning and lies of the egoic mind but able to see their falseness and silliness.

Essence has just as much fun working as it does playing because, when you are in the flow, work is also free of the judgments and self-criticism that usually make work unpleasant. When you are in the egoic state of consciousness and doing something the egoic mind considers work, evaluation is ongoing: You wonder if you are doing it right, well enough, fast enough, soon enough, and as good as so-and-so. You also wonder how others will evaluate it. This, in part, comes from the fact that you were graded throughout school on your performance. Grades, themselves, are a reflection of how the egoic mind sees the world.

This evaluative function is primitive and not as useful as it may seem. It interferes with performance more than it helps because it blocks essence, which is able to perform tasks optimally with minimal support from the mind.

Exercise: Noticing Evaluations

Notice how often you question how well you are doing something while you are doing it. Does this help you perform better or interrupt what you are doing? Where does the answer come from in response to your wondering how you are doing? Is it objective or is it a voice or phrase you have heard before, perhaps from a parent or your usual negative self-talk? Does it even apply to what you are doing now? These evaluative questions and answers usually come from the past and are not relevant to the present.

Notice how the same questions and responses tend to arise no matter what you are doing or how you are doing it. This is conditioning, and it is not helpful. Once you become **aware** of this evaluative voice, you are empowered to ignore it and continue your activity. *The most successful actions arise from a quiet mind, not a busy or evaluative one. Judgments have never improved anyone's performance.*

The egoic mind is so good at sapping the joy out of life that it can even take the joy out of something you love. Even when you are playing, vacationing, being creative, or engaging in a hobby or sport, judgments, comparisons, a hurry-up attitude, or just ordinary thinking can prevent you from enjoying what you are doing. The mind can interfere with enjoyment in so many ways. It pretends to be helpful by offering advice about how to do something or how to do it better or more efficiently. It takes you on mental excursions into the past and future, which may or may not relate to what you are doing. It talks to you throughout an activity, often sounding quite helpful. However, if you listen and engage in conversation with this voice, you will become disengaged from the experience and not enjoy it as fully as possible.

People get used to only partially experiencing life. They dip their toe into experience long enough to feel good enough, without realizing that so much more is possible. *Because there is some enjoyment in thinking, fantasizing, planning, reminiscing, and imagining, this passes as enjoyment and pleasure, especially for those who have developed a more positive mind. Their mind seems like a friend and gives them just enough pleasure to keep them tied to it, never realizing that much more joy is possible.*

The enjoyment provided by the mind is shallow, two-dimensional, and detached from reality. It comes from living in a pretend world, so how real can that enjoyment be? The enjoyment from being truly present in the moment, however, is deeply rich and satisfying because it comes from being in contact with what is Real. It is three-dimensional and vivid, full of aliveness and vibrancy. This is what is possible, but if you keep turning to the mind for pleasure, you won't discover this.

Creativity

You are creators. You are here not only to learn and grow but to create. The Source is using you as its hands, feet, eyes, mouths, and ears to explore the possibilities of creation on this material plane. Without you, it can't manipulate the world or even experience it. It uses your senses to experience the world and your body to manipulate it. The ego also uses your senses and your body to achieve its goals, and much of evolution happens under its grip. However, there comes a time when the Source incarnates through essence and uses the vehicle it has created for its own enjoyment and evolution.

Creativity is not just something that comes through artists, musicians, dancers, and the like, but through everyone who is in touch with essence. Essence is inherently creative. It can't help but create. It takes whatever talents you have and creates. If your talent is business, it expresses its creativity in business. If it is homemaking, it expresses its creativity in that. Whatever your talents are, the potential exists to express them creatively, or as essence would express them.

Creativity is synonymous with being aligned with essence. Essence will use your talents if you allow that. Most of all, this requires trust and letting go of judgment. The key to creativity is just being and allowing essence to move and express itself through you. For this to happen, you have to make room for essence in your life and give it a chance to express itself. The only thing that can stop this and the only thing that ever has stopped this is the egoic mind, in particular judgments and evaluations. Without thought, especially those types of thoughts, there would be only spontaneous action, and that action is ultimately creative.

Essence doesn't act without a purpose. What it does through you serves a purpose, and that purpose is often simply the joy of creating—of bringing something new and different into the world and seeing what impact that has. The joy this creativity brings is the joy of having essence move through you. It is the joy of creating, even more than the joy over the result, although the Source's joy in the result can be felt by you as well.

This is really all anyone wants—to feel this joy of the Creator. It is more fulfilling than anything achieved by the ego for the ego. No amount of money or sensual pleasure can compare to this joy. When you feel it, you know it, and you want to experience it again. The search for this deep joy eventually brings you back to essence. Suffering may get you on the path, but joy is what leads you the rest of the way Home.

This joy of creation can be experienced in very simple ways throughout your day. You don't need to be involved in a grand creative project to feel this. When essence is moving through you, it will be creative in whatever you are doing: cooking, cleaning, gardening, interacting with children, and solving mundane problems. Anything can be fun and rewarding as a result.

To experience creativity in the seemingly insignificant moments, all you need to do is be quiet and respond naturally to what is moving through you. Allow yourself to be a channel for essence in what you are doing and saying. Ignore all useless thoughts about how something should be done and just do, without thinking, and see what happens.

Notice what is arising now...and now...and now. Life is very interesting, very alive, and very dynamic. Every moment is unique. Something is always happening, and often it happens through you. If you are being receptive, you will catch not only what wants to move through you, but what is moving through others. If you are aligned with essence, you will recognize essence being expressed in others and benefit from that. What a joy to see essence everywhere perfectly (although unpredictably) performing this dance of life.

Through you, the Source is busy creating this life, not just for your good, but for the good of all. Its plan is not just for your benefit but for everyone's. When you listen to your call to create, you benefit not only yourself but everyone.

CHAPTER 10
Fulfilling Your Life's Purpose

How Feelings Point to the Flow

When you are aligned with essence, it is easy to tell where the flow is going and, consequently, to discover the path that will be the most satisfying and which will ultimately fulfill your life's purpose. *The direction of the flow is fairly obvious because it is marked by satisfaction, fulfillment, and happiness. These feelings point the way to your life's purpose. When you feel them, you know you are on the right track.*

These good feelings are how essence indicates the direction of the flow and what fits for your life plan. So, if you are following your plan, you will feel good about your life. If you don't feel good about your life, it is wise to question your choices because this may mean they are not aligned with essence's intentions for you.

Discerning this can be a little tricky because if you are enmeshed in the egoic state of consciousness and conditioning, even if you are in the right circumstances to unfold your plan, you may still feel dissatisfied because that is the state of the ego. So, even those who are in the flow in terms of their life plan may not appreciate it because they are not in the flow from moment to moment. Those enmeshed in the egoic state of consciousness are not happy no matter what their circumstances are.

The flow is especially recognizable as happiness. If you are happy, that may be a sign that you are in the flow and aligned with your plan. Not all happiness comes from this, but when it does, it is recognizable and distinct from the happiness of the ego.

You can see the happiness of being aligned with essence in the eyes and demeanor of those experiencing it. It is very attractive. You want to be around them because they seem to have something very special, and they do. Underlying this happiness is calmness, contentment, and peace, which unlike the happiness of the ego, is not dependent on the ups and downs of life. The ego is happy when things go its way, but this feeling fades very quickly.

How Ease Points to the Flow

The flow is also recognizable as ease. When there is ease in your circumstances, you are likely to be in the flow. Within these circumstances, you may not always be in the flow (aligned with essence), but the circumstances, if they feel easy, are likely to be aligned with essence. However, this doesn't mean that if circumstances are not easy that you are not in the flow. Sometimes the flow produces difficult circumstances because they are what you need to grow or develop certain qualities or talents. Nevertheless, ease is a common experience when you are aligned with essence and fulfilling your life's purpose.

This ease may appear as a compatible relationship, a good job, good health, a beautiful home, good friends, help from others, or success. *When you are in the flow and doing what you came here to do, you attract what you need to do that.* For example, if you need to go to school to accomplish your life's purpose, the opportunity will be there. You have to take advantage of that opportunity, but you probably will because it will feel right and good.

In part, this ease comes from the fact that you have helpers who have volunteered to help with your lessons and life's purpose, just as you have volunteered to help with theirs. When your choices are aligned with your life's purpose, these helpers come forward to help you. However, if you are not in circumstances that support your life's purpose, these helpers won't be of much use.

Think of all the times life manifested something beautiful for you through others. They may have been helpers who signed up before this lifetime to help you. These types of agreements are, in part, how the Source brings about its intentions in this dimension.

You probably can think of times when you performed this service for others as well. You were glad to help someone just because it felt right at the moment. These types of agreements can be recognized by their lack of selfishness and self-interest. Help is offered spontaneously (without thinking), cleanly, and gladly because it feels good, not because there is anything in it for you.

This is goodness at work in the world. When this happens, it is good to recognize it. This is actually happening all around you all the time. Take note because the more you notice it, the more you will be made a vehicle for it, which is always very gratifying. This opens the door for more good to come to you as well.

Just as happiness is not always a sign of being aligned with essence and your plan (because it might be the fleeting happiness of the ego), ease is not always a sign either. There are times when ease is present because someone earned that in a previous lifetime, not necessarily because he or she is aligned with the life plan.

If that is the case, the question is, Are they happy? If they are not happy in spite of this ease, it is either because of being identified with the ego or not being aligned with their plan. It is not uncommon for those gifted with ease to wander from their plan because of the many possibilities and choices money provides. This can also result in someone not developing talents or resources that would be in keeping with the plan and which would bring fulfillment and happiness. Ease doesn't necessarily lead to happiness.

Just as ease is not always a sign that you are aligned with your plan, a lack of ease is not always a sign that you are not aligned with your plan. There are a number of reasons why a lack of ease might be present. In this world, work, responsibilities, and difficulties are part of any endeavor. Even when you like your life, you still experience difficulties. Still, some people do seem to have more than their share of difficulties. This may be caused by being a young and inexperienced soul. Their lack of wisdom creates many difficulties that older souls easily avoid because they know better. Difficulties also may be there to provide growth. Challenges evolve you, and the greater the challenge, the greater the possibility for growth.

How Events Point to the Flow

The flow is also recognizable in a series of events. It is often indicated by numerous events or signs pointing in the same direction. For example, let's suppose you are feeling the need for a bigger house. Someone tells you about a new development on the other side of town. A week later, you "happen" to read about it in the paper. A few weeks pass, and you are driving around, when you "happen" upon this new development. You feel excited and call up a realtor. He tells you that a friend of his just found a great house there, and there is one in your price range you might want to look at. You go to see it, fall in love with it, and buy it.

This sounds very ordinary, and it is because the flow is very ordinary. It is how life happens. You are guided by feelings, intuitions, and information coming through others and through other avenues (e.g., books, the internet, and newspapers) to possibilities aligned with essence. *In every moment, essence has an intention for a particular direction. It is willing to have you choose differently, but it makes its intentions known in subtle ways, primarily through your intuition and spontaneous urges and by providing you with information from various places. At times it even speaks to you directly, but more often it drops clues through your intuition and in your environment about possibilities aligned with its intentions for you.*

You can pay attention to these clues or not, but they are there in everyone's life. Following them will lead to greater happiness than other choices. Nevertheless, they are only suggestions, and essence can often fulfill its intentions some other way if you choose to ignore its nudges and promptings. It integrates new suggestions within the life you are creating with your free will. The more open you are to these, the happier you will be and the more likely you will fulfill your lessons and life's purpose.

Even those entrenched in the egoic state of consciousness are able to pick up on these clues if they choose because they are usually very obvious or numerous. Essence shows you the direction of the flow by pointing to it again and again, often until you get it. If you don't, it does the best it can with what you are choosing to create. However, sometimes it doesn't give up so easily and tries through various means to steer you away from your other choices and back to the direction it intends.

Primarily it does this by making certain choices easier than others. That is one way you can tell where the flow is going. *Often the most obvious and easiest choice is the one essence intends, but not always. Unfortunately, there is no formula except to follow your intuition and not your mind.*

Essence also steers you away from a possibility by creating a roadblock to it or by making it unpleasant or difficult once you have chosen it. If nothing is going your way, it is a good idea to question your choices. It may be that you are trying to manifest or have manifested something that is not aligned with essence. *Although sometimes perseverance is the key to success, a lack of success in a particular direction might mean that the direction is not right for you, at least at this time. When this is happening, notice what other opportunities are available to you because the flow will make itself known through other opportunities.*

You don't have to make everything happen, although it feels like that to the ego. Frequently, life just happens easily and effortlessly. These are times of being in the flow. When it is not happening this way, it may be that you are giving too much power to the egoic mind.

The egoic mind is happy to offer ideas about who you are and what you should do with your life. That is its job, but it is incapable of creating a life that will make you happy because its definition of happiness is false. It believes that happiness can be found in power, money, success, fame, beauty, and pleasure, so it sets its goals accordingly. If you follow its ideas, you will have many interesting and challenging experiences, but you won't find a lot of happiness, and the happiness you do find will be fleeting. Even so, learning this is necessary before you are willing to look elsewhere for guidance.

How Longing Points to the Flow

Essence steers you toward possibilities aligned with its goals and away from ones that are not. Sometimes the ego wants something that is not in your best interest to have, but you don't know that. You are convinced you must have that house, that relationship, that job, that car to be happy. How can that not be for you when you feel that way? This is confusing because desires can be very strong. You think that something this strong must be true, but *the strength of a desire is not the measure of its truth. In fact, desires generated by the ego lead you away from fulfillment more often than to it. If you are looking to fulfill your life's purpose, following the ego's desires won't help.*

Desires for specific things, such as a specific relationship, a specific car, or a specific job usually come from and are fed by the ego. The ego imagines what it would be like to have something, and this stirs up feelings, which strengthen the desire. Before you know it, you *have* to have that and you have to have it now. Once the ego decides it wants something, it is very impatient and pushes to make it happen. It doesn't pay attention to what else might be coming out of the flow that could be more fulfilling. It sets its sights on a desire and ignores other possibilities. It limits opportunities by limiting your openness to them because it assumes that what it wants is what is best.

Unlike desires, longings or drives that come from essence are integral to the life plan. They drive the plan forward. You feel them strongly, but they do not originate in the mind. They arise from a deeper place and feel more like a general longing for, for instance, a true love or a home or a fulfilling job or creative expression. These drives don't manifest as specific desires, although they often get attached to a specific desire. When they do and fulfilling that specific desire is not the intention of essence, suffering ensues. This longing is meant to be fulfilled, but not necessarily in the way you think.

Sometimes the longing is there way before it is ready to manifest. This is always difficult, but eventually you learn not to attach this longing to something specific. Rather, you allow it to manifest as it will, in its own time. This is the meaning of surrender—*you surrender your ideas about how your life will unfold to essence's timing and plan, which is being revealed in each moment.* You realize that your mind doesn't know what is best for you. For that, you just have to wait and allow what will be to be and respond in the moment to the longings you feel.

The main difference between longings and desires is that *longings arise in the moment to inspire activity, while desires are based on an idea of what you think you want.* You think something, and a desire arises from that thought. You think: I want a better job (perhaps so that you feel better about yourself), and you follow this up with dreams about what it would be like to have a certain job and possibly with some actions too. This direction may or may not be in keeping with your plan. If it isn't, essence may allow you to pursue it anyway because it may be an opportunity for learning. Sometimes desires do coincide with longings, but the actions that follow might not. It depends on where those actions come from—essence or the ego.

While desires are reflections of thoughts, longings are reflections and signposts of the flow. They point to where the flow is going. Are you longing for a love? If it is coming from essence rather than from the ego, it will be fulfilled sometime. *The longing is a harbinger of what is to come, but you don't know when that will be or what it will look like.* Are you longing for a change in profession? That is the first step in manifesting this change. The longing urges you to take steps to create something new for yourself, but you must take the steps the flow is urging you to take. If this longing is true, you will meet with support and help in taking those steps.

Essence supports the direction it intends. All you need to do is be true to the longings that arise in you. This means you need to be able to discriminate between longing and desire. This is something that develops as you evolve, which is one reason life gets easier the more lifetimes you have lived. The more evolved you are, the less likely you are to follow your desires and lose your way. When you are clear about what is a desire and what is a longing, and you choose to follow your longings rather than your desires, true happiness and fulfillment are much more likely.

Longings are difficult to ignore, but sometimes this happens because of conditioning: What you think you should do interferes with what you long to do. When longings are ignored, the result can be disease, unhappiness, depression, anger, or hopelessness. These may be signs that you are not aligned with essence. They are meant to motivate change, although they don't always succeed. Sometimes others are needed to intervene to show the way. If needed, essence will bring others into your life to facilitate a change of perspective. Therapy often serves this function because it works with conditioning.

Because longings are not easy to ignore, more commonly the problem is that they are misinterpreted as a specific desire for something. This can cause someone to take steps in a direction that doesn't suit the plan. For instance, you feel a longing for a soulmate. Rather than waiting to see what life brings you, you decide to go out and look for someone, but where you look is not where the person who is intended for you is. You meet someone and decide this must be your soulmate, only to find out much later that he or she is not at all right for you. You have spent a great deal of your time and energy involved with the wrong person. Furthermore, while you were involved with this person, you were not open to other possibilities. If essence had intended to arrange a meeting with your soulmate during this time, it would have had to work within the situation you created, which would have been more complicated than if you had been involved with no one.

So much time and energy is spent pursuing goals that are irrelevant to the life's purpose and the intentions of essence. These pursuits have some value as learning tools, but they often take you away from more fulfilling pursuits and may even make finding more fulfilling pursuits more difficult. In taking you in a direction different from where essence would have taken you, these choices often lead to difficulties and pain, not only because they are not fulfilling but because essence may use difficulties to steer you back to its plan. Difficulties get your attention and cause you to question your choices like nothing else, so they are one of the most effective means essence has for communicating its intentions and getting you back on track.

These difficulties could manifest as anything that makes it difficult to get what you want through your current circumstances. Presumably, you created your circumstances because you hoped they would deliver what you want. The ego produced an idea and then a desire and then a plan and followed it, in hopes of creating a situation that would fulfill this desire. If the situation you created fails to do this, the most natural thing is to reevaluate your plan and possibly your desire. Unfortunately, at this point, thinking may still get in the way, and you may create another situation that is still not in keeping with your plan.

As long as you are letting your thoughts and desires determine your goals and actions instead of essence, you may continue to create situations that produce unhappiness and difficulties. When this happens, you may see a pattern and wake up to what is going on, but this can go on for years, decades, even lifetimes before you discover how to live in alignment with essence.

How Excitement Points to the Flow

Just as there are two kinds of desire—that which comes from the ego and that which comes from essence—there are two kinds of excitement. Excitement generated by the ego, as with desires from the ego, is likely to take you away from or interfere with your plan, while excitement generated by essence points the way to the fulfillment of it and your life's purpose.

Excitement that comes from essence arises when something happens that is aligned with your plan or life's purpose. It arises in you suddenly, without thought. This excitement is not created by a thought but is more like a message from essence about what can make you happy. It feels like a yes! and is accompanied by inspiration and a desire for action, not by thoughts about what it means or what is involved or how it will look or what people will say. Those kinds of thoughts are indications that an idea is generated by the ego, not essence, although it is entirely possible for the mind to co-opt essence's inspiration and turn it into an idea and a plan. That happens quite frequently to those who are regularly identified with the ego.

The excitement that arises from essence is like a signal—a flag—that is intended to get you to notice what just took place.

It is like essence giving you a push in a certain direction. It is up to you to do something about that nudge, and that's where it gets tricky. The actions that follow need to come from essence as well, or they may not be in keeping with your plan.

The more you live in the flow and learn to listen to it, the easier your life goes. *Life goes well in direct relationship to how much you attend to essence rather than to the egoic mind.* When you are accustomed to being identified with the ego, however, the instances of essence breaking through and it being allowed to shape your life are few. Nevertheless, the life plan is usually fulfilled one way or another, at least to some extent.

The life plan is broad and not specified before you are born. There are many ways it can be fulfilled, and you get to choose how you will do that. As long as your choices fit the plan to some extent, essence allows them and will not interfere by creating difficulties or roadblocks. However, there are more or less optimal ways that your plan can be fulfilled. Being in touch with essence will lead you to fulfill your plan in a way that will bring the greatest satisfaction and happiness. If you fulfill it some other way, it may be less satisfying and bring you less happiness than is possible.

This is the situation many find themselves in. They are fulfilling their plan but not using their potentials and resources optimally. They also may not be making use of their helpers as they might. The more closely you are aligned with essence, the more your helpers are able to serve you as intended. A looser alignment might make their help irrelevant. For example, if someone who is an excellent professor made a pre-life agreement to help you become a better teacher in this lifetime, and you end up teaching elementary school (which may still fulfill your plan to some extent), the professor's skills wouldn't be of much help.

Excitement is used at every step to show you the way to fulfillment. If a direction is right for you, you will feel excitement arise when you learn about it. Then, when you take steps toward making that happen, you will feel excited at each step. Any ideas you have about how this should look or how you should go about it will only get in the way. Following this excitement and not being waylaid by your ideas or your conditioning will take you in a fulfilling direction. No one knows what will make you happy better than essence. Fulfilling its intentions is the only thing that will really provide the happiness you are looking for.

How Opportunities Point to the Flow

Some of the most important and obvious pointers to fulfillment are opportunities. Life is full of them. Opportunities are always presenting themselves: People suggest you do this or go here or read this book or apply for this job or sign up for this course. They offer you money, help, advice, and friendship. These smaller opportunities often lead to bigger ones that ultimately fulfill your life's purpose. So, it is important not to overlook the little opportunities because a little opportunity may be the first step on a very fulfilling path.

It is easy to overlook opportunities. The ego may discount an opportunity because it doesn't like the person offering it or something else about the situation. It has judgments about everything, and these interfere with noticing the blessings life offers through others and in other ways. The egoic mind is so busy thinking about itself and judging that it doesn't notice the messages being sent by essence. Even when it does, it often comes up with reasons not to pay attention to them.

When opportunities are not taken advantage of, essence continues to offer them, perhaps in other ways and through other people. Repetition of the message is often what finally breaks through the egoic trance. Repetition makes it more likely that you will stop thinking long enough to pay attention to your feelings in considering an opportunity. That is when essence expresses itself as happiness and excitement, which may motivate you to take advantage of the opportunity.

How People Point to the Flow

Essence expresses itself through others and may express itself through anyone. However, there are those whose life purpose is to provide spiritual guidance. Astrologers, psychics, channels, spiritual counselors, and others who offer themselves in service to other people's growth and understanding are entrusted with the task of helping others find their way. They are not infallible, but many are very helpful. Although you need to be discriminating in selecting one and taking his or her advice, talking to someone who comes highly recommended may bring clarity or help you trust what you intuitively know.

You should never come away from a spiritual counselor, psychic, channel, or astrologer feeling bad about yourself or fearful about your future. If this happens, he or she is not a worthy messenger. These individuals are learning too, and some are at the beginning stages of their apprenticeship and may not realize yet how much they don't know.

It is very easy for intuition and psychic gifts to get corrupted by the ego. The more identified with the ego the person is, the less helpful his or her insights and advice are likely to be. Those who are operating at a high level in this area are dedicated to their own personal and spiritual growth and committed to being aligned with essence. When searching for a spiritual advisor, let a lack of ego-identification be your guide. Experience is also important, but not as important as pure intent, commitment to serving humanity, and alignment with essence.

You should come away from a session feeling uplifted, inspired, and positive about yourself and about life. What is said about your life plan and purpose should coincide with your intuition and other signposts. It should confirm and validate what you know on a deepest level to be true about you and why you are here—because *you do know why you are here.* You may not trust that you know and you may feel confused about it, but you do know. What they say should confirm this knowing, and that should feel very good.

How Intuition Points to the Flow

The egoic mind can't point you in the direction of fulfillment because it doesn't know what will fulfill you. Fortunately, you don't need to rely on the mind to know this. You were given intuition to provide the moment-to-moment guidance you need to get you there.

Intuition is something that develops over time by using it, but it is active within everyone to some extent and more active the more you listen to it. Your intuition points you to the messages and opportunities arising in the flow related to your life's purpose. It tells you to pay attention to something someone said or did, or to go here or go there, or to do this or do that, all of which take you where you need—and want—to go. By following your intuition in each moment, the life you were meant to live is revealed.

Intuition is the alternative to the egoic mind. *When you stop listening to the mind, what is left is your intuition, which arises in between the thoughts.* Catch it there because not only will it take you back to essence but to your greatest fulfillment—your life's purpose.

Intuition arises within you suddenly, like a flash, an inspiration. Sometimes it feels like information has just been downloaded into your body, and you just *know* something. Trust this. It is really very simple when you get used to this happening. When you pay attention to it, it happens more often. Eventually intuitions will arise nearly as often as thoughts to guide you on your way. They eventually replace thought as a way of moving through life. Thoughts quiet down, and intuitions become louder and easier to catch and more difficult to ignore. Before, the mind was difficult to ignore, now intuitions can't be ignored.

Along with intuitions, ideas pop into your mind out of nowhere. *Ideas that come from essence have an impact—you notice them. They drop or pop into your mind and often feel surprising. There is a clarity and power about them. You know they are right, and you act on them. These ideas are very direct pointers to what you need to do to be aligned with your plan and life's purpose.* If you can be true to them, you will find yourself living in the flow more and more because they will keep you busy unfolding your life from essence, not from ego.

Summary: Pointers to the Flow and Your Life's Purpose

1. Feelings of satisfaction, fulfillment, happiness, peace, contentment
2. Easeful circumstances, liking your life
3. Help from others that supports a certain direction
4. A series of events pointing to the same thing
5. A deep longing
6. Excitement over some possibility
7. Opportunities, doors opening in a certain direction
8. Information/advice from people, including channels, astrologers, and psychics
9. Intuition, a knowing, an inspiration, a sudden flash or idea

---

Fulfilling Your Destiny

Most people who are not in the flow much of the time still fulfill their life purpose, at least to some extent, because of the abundant pointers and because the drive to do that is so compelling. To be happy and fulfilled, you don't have to be in the flow continually; you just have to visit it and listen to it enough to catch its direction and follow that.

Every lifetime has a different life purpose. However, it is not uncommon for a soul to have a series of related or similar life purposes because that is how proficiency and talents are built. The talents you have were not just given to you through birth, for instance. You developed them in previous lifetimes and then chose an environment that would nurture them or perhaps provide a catalyst for their development.

Whatever your circumstances are in this life, they can serve you. Whether they do this or not depends on your attitude toward them. Anyone can learn to make lemons out of lemonade. You can't change the circumstances you were born into or the challenges you were given or what you have already created, but you can learn to manage how you think about all of this.

Your thoughts (the ones you are identified with and believe) determine your experience of reality. *You can't change what is or what has been, but you can change how you think about it. You can choose to tell a positive story rather than a negative story about it, or you can choose to tell no story at all.*

This is self-mastery. *How you respond to experience is the only thing you can truly control.* That is where your free will is really free to choose. You can choose to give up trying to control life. You can decide to allow and accept—and enjoy—whatever is happening rather than fight against it, feel victimized by it, complain about it, or blame someone for it. You can choose to say yes to whatever is happening. This allows you to float down this river of life without suffering. By just saying yes to it all, you can enjoy the ride the Source is taking you on and experiencing through you.

This attitude doesn't lead to complacency or passivity—on the contrary. The flow will use you as you were meant to be used. It will take you where it wants you to be—and you will like it! You can't help but be happy when you are in the flow because you were meant to have certain experiences and achieve certain goals. Doing this is inherently rewarding, regardless of what those experiences or goals may be.

You were meant for this life you are having, not some other life, not someone else's life. The ego doesn't understand this. It wants all the goodies, without realizing that what it might consider bad is a goodie too. It is all good, and you are here to experience it.

Experiencing is the reason you are here. However, you are not here for just any experience but for the ones you are having because *you are the only one in this entire universe destined for these experiences.* They are designed just for you. You are co-creating them with the Source, which is loving it all. It is a blessing, indeed, to have this opportunity to be alive in these magnificent times. Be in joy!

ABOUT THE AUTHOR

Gina Lake has a Masters degree in Counseling Psychology. Since 1984, she has used this and her knowledge of astrology to help people understand their spiritual lessons and life purpose. She is also a conscious channel and uses this to support and facilitate spiritual awakening. She is the author of several books about spirituality, including *Radical Happiness: A Guide to Awakening; Anatomy of Desire: How to Be Happy Even When You Don't Get What You Want; Choosing Love: A Guide to Spiritual Relationship;* and *Symbols of the Soul: Discovering Your Karma Through Astrology.* She also compiled and edited *Nothing Personal: Seeing Beyond the Illusion of a Separate Self* based on the teachings of her husband, Nirmala, which are about awakening and self-realization. Together they offer satsang gatherings and retreats.

Excerpts from these books are available on Gina's website: **www.radicalhappiness.com**. *Nothing Personal* and other publications by Nirmala are available as free downloads from his website: **www.endless-satsang.com**. Nirmala is also available for consultations. All proceeds from their books and consultations go to Endless Satsang Foundation, a non-profit organization. They can be reached by email at **ginalakenow@aol.com** and **nirmalanow@aol.com**.

Printed in the United States
98785LV00009B/68/A